The House of Bernarda Alba

Federico García Lorca was born in 1898 near Granada, the son of a wealthy farmer. He studied in the Faculties of Arts and Law at the provincial university before moving to the Residence for Students, a prestigious college in Madrid, during a period of intellectual and artistic ferment. He travelled in the USA and South America in 1929 and 1930, and in 1931 was made director of the touring theatre La Barraca by the Republican government of Spain. He was murdered by Nationalist partisans in 1936. He published several books of poetry: *Book of Poems* (1921), *Songs* (1927), *Gypsy Ballads* (1928), *Poem of Deep Song* (1931) and *First Songs* (1936). His stage plays include: *The Butterfly's Evil Spell* (1920), *Mariana Pineda* (1927), *The Shoemaker's Wonderful Wife* (1930), *Blood Wedding* (1933), *The Love of Don Perlimplín* (1933), *Yerma* (1934), *When Five Years Pass* (rehearsed reading, 1936) and *The House of Bernarda Alba* (private reading, 1936).

Rona Munro has written extensively for stage, radio, film and television including the award winning plays *Iron*, *Bold Girls* and *The Maiden Stone*. Other plays include *Long Time Dead* produced by Paines Plough Theatre Company and *The Indian Boy* produced by the Royal Shakespeare Company and adaptations *Mary Barton* and *Watership Down* which were produced by Manchester Royal Exchange Theatre and the Lyric Hammersmith. Film and television work includes the Ken Loach film *Ladybird Ladybird*, *Aimee and Jaguar* and television dramas *Rehab* and BAFTA nominated *Bumping The Odds* for the BBC. She has also written many other single plays for radio and television and contributed to series such as *Casualty* and *Dr Who*.

D1151321

Also available from Methuen Drama
by Federico García Lorca

Methuen Student Editions

Blood Wedding
Doña Rosita the Spinster
The House of Bernarda Alba
Yerma

Collected Volumes

LORCA PLAYS: ONE
(Blood Wedding, Doña Rosita the Spinster, Yerma)

LORCA PLAYS: TWO
(The Shoemaker's Wonderful Wife, The Love of Don Perlimplin,
The Puppet Play of Don Christóbel, The Butterfly's Evil Spell,
When Five Years Pass)

LORCA PLAYS: THREE
(Mariana Pineda, The Public, Play without a Title)

Federico García Lorca

The House of Bernarda Alba

a modern adaptation by
Rona Munro

**NATIONAL
THEATRE
OF SCOTLAND**

Methuen Drama

Published by Methuen Drama 2009

1 3 5 7 9 10 8 6 4 2

Methuen Drama
A & C Black Publishers Limited
36 Soho Square
London W1D 3QY
www.methuendrama.com

A CIP catalogue record for this book is available from the British Library

ISBN: 978 1 408 12696 7

Typeset by Country Setting, Kingsdown, Kent
Printed and bound in Great Britain by
CPI Cox & Wyman Ltd, Reading, Berkshire

The House of Bernarda Alba

The House of Bernarda Alba in this version was first presented at the Citizens Theatre, Glasgow, on 17 September 2009, by the National Theatre of Scotland, and subsequently toured to the Dundee Rep Theatre, the Alhambra Theatre, Dunfermline, and the King's Theatre, Edinburgh. The cast was as follows:

Marty	Louise Ludgate
Agnes	Julie Wilson Nimmo
Melly	Carmen Pieraccini
Bernie	Siobhan Redmond
Adie	Vanessa Johnson
Maggie	Jo Freer
Penny	Myra McFadyen
Mary	Una McLean
Careworker	Anne Lacey
Prudence / Churchgoer	Mary McCusker
1st Journalist	Morag Stark
2nd Journalist	Heather Nimmo

Director John Tiffany
Designer Laura Hopkins
Lighting Designer Natasha Chivers
Sound Designer Paul Arditti

Characters

Bernie
Agnes
Marty
Melly
Adie
Maggie
Mary
Penny
Prue
Careworker
Churchgoer
1st Journalist
2nd Journalist

Scene One

The front room of **Bernie***'s house.*

Ambulance and police sirens sound insistently in the distance.

The **Careworker** *enters.*

Careworker Those sirens are giving me a headache.

Penny *enters. She's swigging from a bottle.*

Penny Six hours of that racket. Busies all over the scheme.
Do you think there's anyone this side of the city that doesn't
know what's happening? Maggie keeled over when the police
escort pulled up outside.

Careworker She's going to feel this.

Penny She's the only one who will. Daddy's girl, eh? God
help her. (*She drinks.*) Oh, this is good! Thank Christ for five
minutes' peace. I'll need a bit of sugar to get through the next
few hours.

Careworker If Bernie sees you . . .

Penny Oh aye, right, like she won't need a wee something
for the 'shock'. Well, I've had a jolt too. Sod her. I'm missing
lunch for this. They'll all be back in a minute. I need to keep
my strength up.

Careworker Is that . . . champagne?

Penny (*offering it*) Freixenet. Go through and get another
one. Have you ever been offered as much as a cup of tea any
visit? I reckon she owes you, don't you?

A voice off, **Mary***.*

Mary (*off*) Bernadette!

Penny Oh Christ, don't tell me the old crocodile's waking
up.

Careworker It's OK. She's had her prescription. I watched
her swallow it.

Penny   You ask me you should up the dose. If you ask me you should hide her teeth while you're about it.

Mary   Bernadette!

Penny (*calling*)   She'll be with you in a minute, Mary! (*To* **Careworker**.) Listen, if Bernie finds her out her bed at a time like this –

Careworker   Well, none of this is that poor old soul's fault. It's not her fault she hasn't the first clue what's going on. No one speaks to her except me. No one even looks in on her. You know what?

Penny   What?

Careworker   I know I shouldn't at a time like this but . . .

Penny   You can say it.

Careworker   Well, truth is I can't stand that Bernie Alba. I'm starting to really dislike the woman.

Penny   What took you so long? She's like a dose of weedkiller on a pot of primroses. She just blights any life she touches. She'd put poison in your food one wee drop at a time and give herself a year's entertainment watching you die by inches.

Penny *looks at the bottle for a second, then puts the remnants down.*

Careworker   I mean, I'm usually pretty good at not letting a client's family situation get to me, but this lot . . .

Penny   They are something else, aren't they? And her? Sleekit. She knew this was coming. Don't tell me she didn't know. She just didny know when.

She wants it all. And she gets it.

Lording it over everyone else on the road with her new car and a flat screen even in the cludgie but, oh, she's still a poor soul that has to fight for every penny the social services grudge her.

I even believe it when she gets going.

Careworker (*looking round*) But they're . . . !

Penny Loaded. Aye. Tell me about it.

It's not real money, though, is it? Not money in the bank. Not money on paper anywhere you could ever find it. His money.

Careworker Who'll get it now?

Penny Whoever can find it. The court will be after it unless they find another washing machine to chuck it into.

Another burst of sirens, passing and fading away. **Penny** *looks round the edge of the window.*

Careworker Will they all come back here?

Penny No. There was going to be a send-off in the club but the police put a stop to that. Don't think Bernie's worried. Saved her a hell of a drinks bill.

Careworker (*alarmed*) The police are coming here?

Penny Just to the door. They won't come in here till they've got a warrant or an invite. Bernie's got pet lawyers on speed dial. The police don't get into her lair if those boys can help it. The press now, that's a different matter. That doorbell's going to be ringing all night.

Careworker I don't know what I'm supposed to do here . . .

Penny Your job.

Careworker How long have you worked for them?

Penny Thirty years.

She sees the **Careworker***'s reaction.*

Penny I know. I was at school with Bernie. Girls together. (*Pause.*) She was beautiful, you know. Absolutely beautiful – it would have tugged the heart out of you. So young. We both were. Thirty years of drying her tears and holding the babies while she cried. Helping her up the prison for the visits, taking her in my own car.

Careworker She's got two cars now.

Penny   We were close back then. I thought she was a wee snowdrop Tony Alba had snatched out the ground to squash in his big red fist. I thought she was young love pulled to her knees in all his shit.

Pause.

Careworker   Thirty years.

Penny   Aye.

Careworker   You never fancied another job?

Penny   Pub work suits me. (*Pause.*) I thought she needed me. Now . . . I've watched that wee trophy bride turn as hard and brassy as the chains round Tony Alba's neck. I've swallowed her lies and they've poisoned me, so I think compassion's a mug's game, a trick played on the good-hearted by the rest of the wicked world. Oh aye, Bernie's had my hope, digested that years ago in a sauce of crocodile tears. This could be the end of her. And I'll get to watch.

Careworker   The end of her?

Penny   How's she going to keep the 'business' going with Tony gone? (*Laughs.*) And her with five great girls all stuck here at home.

Careworker   Why?

Penny   Why what?

Careworker   Why are they all stuck here?

Penny   Because that's what Bernie wants. They're what she does when Tony's doing what he does. Like an indoor cat with a scratching post. And now Tony's gone.

Oh yeah, you're juggling with gelignite there, Bernie, aren't you?

He put half the business in Agnes's name, years ago. That's the only legitimate money Bernie could get her hands on, but it's in Agnes's name. Did it to save his assets. (*Laughs.*) Agnes has got the assets now.

Careworker   Why Agnes?

Penny   She's the eldest.

She's not Tony's. Not blood. Works better for the fraud
investigators. When Tony chucked out Mrs Alba number one,
Agnes moved in with Bernie as part of the package. Bernie
used to tell folk Agnes was her little sister. Nae wonder Agnes
is screwed up.

Careworker   But the house and the club . . . ?

Penny   Oh, Bernie'll keep this.

Careworker   It's some size, this place.

Penny   Well, to be fair, there's the club downstairs and seven
of them in here. There was eight till last week.

Careworker   What I mean is . . . my house isny this nice.

Penny   I bought mine. Couldny give it away now of course.
Wrong end of the scheme.

Careworker   Rent or mortgage. You give your whole lives
to bricks and mortar, don't you? If I didny get a week in
Spain once a year I'd go –

Penny (*interrupts*)   Bernie's got a villa in Spain.

Careworker   For real?

Penny   Oh, not *official*. Not on paper. But it's theirs. Swimming
pool. Terracotta tiles. Vine growing over the outside dining
area. I've seen photos.

Careworker   And I'm in there wiping her mother's arse
three times a day, that can't be right. How is it no some agency
nurse getting crabbit shit under her finger nails!

Penny   Welcome to my world.

A car outside. Blue flashing police lights light up the room.

Penny   They're back. (*Looking out of the window.*) Two cars.
Oh, it's that detective sergeant with the shoulders, have you
seen him? They should set him walking the streets. Just makes

you feel safe to look at him. Swaggers like Clint Eastwood, like he can put the world to rights just by fixing it with a straight stare from those bright blue eyes. Truth is he probably couldny even catch a blind junkie with no soles on her trainers but those shoulders make you feel safe. Course we'll never see the like of Sergeant Tavendale, mind him? No, before your time. Used to bring me back to Mum by the ear when I'd been lifting fizzy cola chews from Woolies. He just had to raise his arm – (*demonstrates*) and the kids scattered behind their front doors and slammed them shut on all their badness. Not that he'd've whacked us for real of course . . . but the idea of it was a comfort somehow – a strong right arm to keep the kids in line. How does that not work any more?

Careworker   The kids have got guns.

Penny   I knew there was a reason. See you in a minute.

Penny *exits.*

The **Careworker** *looks a bit lost for a moment, then she starts to poke around, looking at family photos, picking up expensive knick-knacks, tutting at their extravagance.*

The **Churchgoer** *inches round the door.*

Churchgoer (*very quiet*)   I . . . I've come to help.

The **Careworker** *is examining a Doulton figure, peering at the maker's name. She doesn't hear or see the* **Churchgoer**.

Churchgoer (*coughs*)   I've come to help?

The **Careworker** *startles, the china goes flying. It smashes. They both look at it.*

Careworker   That was fucking Royal Doulton.

Churchgoer   I'm sorry.

The **Careworker** *stares at the pieces a moment then she sighs and starts to gather them up.*

Churchgoer   The door was open. I heard about your trouble. I've come to help.

Careworker I just work here. They're on their way in. Did you not see them out there?

Churchgoer Yes, I . . . I just thought . . .

Careworker What?

Churchgoer I'm from the church. St Magdalene's? Mrs Alba comes to our mass.

Careworker Does she now?

Churchgoer I'm from the bereavement counselling group. I heard about Mr Alba.

Careworker You and the whole scheme.

Churchgoer Sorry?

Careworker So even the church wants a look at the bullet holes, does it? Buy a paper like everyone else.

Churchgoer . . . Mr Alba was *shot*?

Careworker You're no really from here, are you? It was a shoot-out at the Stallion Club. Did you no hear the sirens? Four of his boys were still holed up in there for hours. Then they torched the place. Did you not see the smoke? It was all over the telly! You knew Tony Alba?

Churchgoer He . . . he came to mass.

Careworker Did he now?

Anyway, I don't think this is a good time.

Churchgoer No, perhaps I should . . .

Careworker I mean, I'm here, the woman that works for them's here. That's the police bringing the family home. They've got professional help, you know?

Churchgoer Yes. Maybe I should call again in a few weeks.

Careworker (*still picking up china*) Aye, you do that.

The **Churchgoer** *exits. The* **Careworker** *clears up, muttering to herself.*

Careworker   Oh, so Tony Alba went to church did he?
God, I'd love to have been a wee slater in the skirting board
of that confessional. Did you tell the priest where you picked
up the Royal Doulton then, Tony? There'll be camera crews
all over the scheme again, won't there? We'll all switch on our
televisions and every poor decent soul trying to keep it together
in flats with no lifts at the tail end of all the bus routes will get
another wee reminder that we're all hoods and wasters down
here, eh? They'll get a good shot through the nets at the
Royal Doulton and the plasma screen and everyone'll be
marvelling about what folk can afford on the social. Who'd
be the deserving poor? The undeserving hoods make so much
of a song and dance no one even knows we're here. I tell you,
Mr Alba, I'm glad you ended up lying full of bullets on a shelf
in a fridge. One less bit of dirt to stick to the rest of us.

Bernie *has entered at the tail end of this muttered rant.*

She is in tight, glamorous black.

The **Careworker** *sees her.*

Careworker   Oh, Mrs Alba, I'm so sorry for your loss.

Bernie (*sees the broken china*)   What have you done?

Careworker   It was this woman from the church, Mrs
Alba, she just walked in. I didn't . . .

Bernie   Are you paid to sit around on my settee or are you
paid to take care of my mother?

Behind **Bernie** *a procession is filing into the room: her five daughters,
also in fashionable mourning, and a small posse of press.*

Careworker   I'm really sorry, Mrs Alba, I just . . .

Bernie   Tony gave me that! Get out! Go on! Go and do
what they pay you for!

The **Careworker** *hurries out.*

Bernie (*shaking with anger*)   Maggots. Parasites the lot of
them.

Journalist 1   That was your . . . ?

Bernie   She's my mother's careworker. Just one of the leeches sucking this family dry.

Journalist 2   But . . . isn't she here to help you look after – ?

Bernie   Did I ask your opinion? Did I? (*To* **Journalist 1**) Who is this?

She gives her colleague a warning glare. **Journalist 2** *backs off.*

Journalist 1   I'm sorry, Bernie. She doesn't know what you've been going through.

Bernie   She knows I lost my husband of thirty years, doesn't she?

Behind them **Maggie** *starts to cry.*

Bernie   Aw Maggie, please, if you can't stop, can you take it out of the room? We're worn out with this. Maggie, stop it!

Maggie's *tears subside.*

Journalist 1   Are you all right to do this, Bernie?

Bernie   I said I'd give you an exclusive, didn't I? You get a taste and the rest of them have to leave the flesh on our bones. That's the deal. Keep them off us.

Penny *is looking round the edge of the curtain again.*

Penny   There's two more camera crews out there.

Bernie   Penny, go and tell them, tell them we're going exclusive. Tell them they're wasting their time.

Penny   Since when did I become your personal assistant?

Bernie   Oh, for the love Christ, Penny, they won't take your picture will they?! Go and tell them. Tell them to fuck right – (*checks herself*) to give us peace. (*Quietly.*) And tell him thanks for putting the dogs out there on the gate, Penny. We'll manage ourselves now, tell him

Journalist 2   Are those the Romanovs' dogs out there?

Agnes   Yes.

Penny *exits.*

Bernie (*same time*)   No! I don't know. A neighbour lent them to me. To keep the other dogs off us. A kindness. That's all.

Journalist 2   Mr Romanov was an associate of your husband, wasn't he?

Agnes   They were business part –

Bernie (*cutting **Agnes** off*)   They knew each other. They had occasional contact. As acquaintances. As members of the same business community.

Journalist 2   It's just I thought I saw them drinking together. At the Stallion Club. Last week, this was.

Bernie *studies her for a moment.*

Bernie   Well, honey, there's only two kinds of girls get into the Stallion Club, so either you were doing a wee lap dance or you're sucking on some footballer to get yoursel a free margarita, so which is it?

The **Crew** *setting up the lights and camera exchange looks, wincing.*

Marty (*quietly*)   Right between the eyes.

Bernie   Something you need to say, girls?

Penny *is back in.*

Penny (*warning*)   Camera's on, Bernie.

Journalist 1   Just if you're ready, Bernie.

Bernie *goes still, looking down. Emotion seems to wash over her. The lights go on, camera is steadied.*

Bernie (*quietly*)   Girls . . .

Silently the five women gather round their mother on the settee, grouping themselves as if rehearsed.

Bernie *looks up into the camera lens.*

Journalist 1   Mrs Alba, I know this must be a very difficult time for you.

Bernie   Yes.

Journalist 1   Have you any idea who may have killed your husband?

Bernie   I appeal to the police. I appeal to the public. If anyone has any information, please, please come forward.

Journalist 1   You had no idea your husband was involved with the kind of men who gunned him down?

Bernie   I can't believe he was. I won't believe he was. My husband was a good man and a loving father . . .

She can't go on.

Journalist 1   How are you feeling now, Bernie?

Bernie   We're all just devastated. We're in shock. I'm sorry, I can't . . .

Bernie *clings to* **Melly***'s hand for support, nearly breaking down.* **Maggie** *is crying again.*

Journalist 1   Is there anything else you'd like to say, Bernie?

Bernie   I'd just like to ask the media to please respect my family's privacy. Give us peace. Let us grieve.

She looks straight to camera again, then bows her head. A pause, then the light goes off.

Journalist 1   Thanks, Bernie, we'll get out of your hair now.

The crew start to pack up quickly. **Bernie** *stays where she is, all her daughters leaning into her and on each other.*

Journalist 2   I'm sorry, OK? I really am.

Bernie *nods without looking at her.*

The crew is exiting. **Penny** *looks round the curtains.*

Penny   Most of them are moving off.

Journalist 2 *passes her card to* **Maggie**, *who's still crying.*

Journalist 2   If you ever need to talk. I am sorry.

She exits with the rest. As soon as she's gone **Bernie** *snatches the card off* **Maggie** *and tears it.*

Agnes *slips out quietly after the* **Journalists**.

Marty *is fixing herself a drink.*

Bernie   Aye, clear out the lot of you. Crawl back down the sewers and tear me to bits. You'll not get past my door again. (*To* **Maggie**.) Stop it, Maggie! You're splitting my head!

Penny   They've paid you though, eh?

Bernie   We'll be lucky if it covers the funeral. God, I can smell them. (*Sprays air-freshener around.*) Hyena sweat, vulture breath.

Melly   Mum, don't, please don't . . .

Bernie   They're sorry for my loss, are they? Sorry for their own loss more like. Nothing left here but bones for them to suck on. They'll have to work a bit harder for their headlines, won't they? Spin their lies out of someone else's heartache.

Penny   There's a wee posse still out there. Cameras ready.

Bernie   Draw the curtains, Penny. They'll have their lenses through the nets. God, I'm dry.

Adie   I'll get you a cup of tea, Mum.

Bernie   A cup of tea? *A cup of tea?* Mother of God, I've just buried my husband! Get me a drink!

Marty *hands* **Bernie** *her own drink.*

Marty   That's the last of the vodka.

Bernie   What about you?

Marty   I'm all right.

Bernie   Well, this'd be a good time to get up to Asda. Stock up. Get Penny to take you. Stock up on everything. Go round

and check all the window locks are on. Then we'll put the
security lights on and sit it out. I don't want any of you putting
a foot round that door until I say so. We'll sit the bastards out.
I've played this game before. I know what I'm doing.

Adie   We can't just stay locked up till –

Bernie   Aw, and where would you be going anyway, honey?
There's none of your sisters had the gumption to get themselves
a man or a job or a life outside this scheme so I doubt you're
any different. Stay home and let Mammy pay the bills, eh?
Well, you can all start thinking about economising now, can't
you? There'll be no Saturday mornings up the town for any
of you. No nights out at the club, no one to pay off all that
hot plastic. What's the odds of any of you lot making your
own way in the world? Here's the news. You'll all have to live
off beans on toast and Oxfam cardies for the rest of your
days. Start getting used to it. Start shifting yourself to be
useful round here. Maggie'll show you how.

Maggie   Eh? How does that work?

Adie   She means you can show us how to guilt-trip the
world running around making soup and ironing Dad's shirts
like a live-in maid.

Maggie   Don't you talk about Dad . . . don't you . . .

Bernie (*interrupting*)   You dare! You *dare*! *I'm* the one who's
heartbroken here! *I'm* the one . . .

She can't go on.

Maggie   I never wanted to stay home. I never wanted that.

Bernie   So why didn't you shift yourself somewhere else?!
Well, you're stuck here now, lassie. You all are. No one's going
to be paying for wee jaunts abroad or a new set of wheels
now. I've only made it five miles from the hole I was born into
and none of you have half the strength I did. Welcome home
for the rest of your whinging lives! Get used to it!

Take that look off your face, Maggie. Daddy's no here to take
your part now, is he?

Adie *leaves the room.* **Mary** *calls off.*

Mary (*off*)   Bernadette! Let me out!

Bernie (*shouting off*)   What are you doing to her?

The **Careworker** *enters looking really flustered, nursing her arm.*

Careworker   I can't do this, Mrs Alba. I really don't have to put up with this.

Bernie   She bit you, did she? (*Laughs.*) God love her, she's no dead yet, is she?

Careworker   Mrs Alba, I know this probably isn't the time but I'm responsible for your mother's health. She is starved of attention. Her mental health is deteriorating. She is malnourished and disorientated.

Marty   She puts it on half the time, you know.

Bernie   Open all her windows. Let her get some fresh air.

Careworker   She's through there putting on a backless evening dress and stilettos. She says she's got a hot date.

The women look at each other, stifling giggles.

Bernie   Let her feel the breeze. Don't let her lean out, though.

Careworker   Why? Do you think she's after jumping?

Bernie   No. I don't want some bugger with a telephoto getting a shot of her.

The **Careworker** *exits.*

Marty   I'm going up to change.

Bernie   I don't want you slobbing about in some track suit, Marty. If they see us we need to look sharp. Mind you, track suit says grief, doesn't it . . . ? OK, wear what you like, but stay away from the windows.

Adie *comes back in.*

Bernie   Where's Agnes?

Adie   She's looking onto the back green. There's a camera crew talking to our neighbours across the way.

Bernie   And what were you doing looking out?

Adie   I was checking the window locks! Like you told us!

Bernie   She's looking at a *camera crew*?!

Adie   I don't know. The Romanov boys are out there. Walking the dogs.

Bernie (*furious*)   Agnes! Agnes get in here!

Agnes (*running in, startled*)   What? What's happened?

Bernie   What were you looking at? *Who* were you looking at?

Agnes   Nothing. No one.

Bernie   Your father's blood's still warm on the pavement and you're out there winking at the world, are you?

Agnes   I wasn't! I –

Bernie   What do you think you're playing at?

Agnes   He wasn't my father. And someone's got to look out for the business now, don't they?

Bernie *hits her.*

Bernie   Oh you *poisonous* bit of sugar you!

Penny *jumps in.*

Penny   Bernie! Calm down!

She restrains **Bernie**.

Bernie   Get out! Go to your rooms! All of you!

Everyone exits except **Bernie** *and* **Penny**.

Penny (*stroking* **Bernie**, *soothing her*)   She didn't mean it, Bernie. She doesn't have it in her to be scheming or two-faced. She's thinking about taking some responsibility. She's thinking it's down to her now.

Bernie   Aw for God's sake, she doesny have a clue.

Penny   No.

Bernie   Was it the Romanov boys out there?

Penny   A few of them. Yes.

Bernie   What are they up to?

Penny   They won't be bothering you.

Bernie   What do you know? (*As* **Penny** *hesitates.*) Aw, come on, Penny, this is you and me now.

Penny   What I heard is it's some bother with Rosie Kennedy's man.

Bernie   In too deep, is he? What did they do?

Penny   Took a bat to him, tied him up and had Rosie on the settee in front of him.

Bernie   Aw, God help her . . .

Penny   She opened the door to them.

Bernie   Serious?!

Penny   Way I heard it you could hear her laughing on the ground floor. She left with them.

Bernie   What do you mean, she left with them?

Penny   What do you think I mean? She was off down the stairs between the three of them with her tits still hanging out, giggling her head off.

Bernie   Hell mend her. You could tell that one was going down the devil's toilet, eh?

Penny   If she'd been living round here this last while she might have thought twice about that change of location. She doesn't know what the Romanovs are like. She thinks they're like her usual pick-ups, so grateful for a blow job they'll keep her in stockings and sangria as long as she fancies. She's fucked this time. Every way you want to look at it.

Bernie   It's all going to kick off now Tony's gone, isn't it?

Penny   Well . . . that's maybe what Agnes was thinking of. Thinking about what to do.

Bernie   *Agnes* thinking about what to do?! She doesn't have a clue, Penny! She doesn't have the first idea! You know what she's been up to this last while? Business management courses! At the college. She thinks she can run Tony's business by learning people skills and mastering Windows fucking Vista! They'll eat us up and ask us to pass the ketchup. Oh dear God, we're not going to know what's hit us, Penny. And there's no one can hold the tide back but me.

Penny   Och well. Least you've got your family round you, eh?

Bernie   (*smelling the sarcasm*)   What have you got your spoon into now?

Penny   Just what I said. You must be glad you've got them all home. Though mebbe . . .

Bernie   What?

Penny   Mebbe now Tony's gone it's a chance for everyone to move on.

Bernie   Move on? What do you mean? Move on?

Penny   Well, Marty was bright enough for college.

Bernie   And it nearly killed her. Couldny hack it, could she? Face down in the student bedsit with her belly full of barbiturates in case you'd forgotten – she's no strong enough without me behind her, you know that.

Penny   Well, OK, but Melly could –

Bernie   *What?* Get hersel a nice wee hairdressing job? How many of those did she try before she ended up with her fat arse plonked back on my settee? I've got to carry them, Penny, I've got to carry them all. I'll do it, they're my blood and bones, but I know they'll never thank me.

Penny   All right. Wee Adie . . .

Bernie   Is a *child*.

Penny   You had Agnes at her age.

Bernie   And that's what I'll save her from.

Penny   OK, so this isn't the time for this conversation.

Bernie   They are not going to do what I did. They are not going to grab some man they think is hard enough to keep them safe and then spend the rest of their days worrying about every knock on the door.

Penny   They could get a life, Bernie!

Bernie   Do you see any of that bunch managing that?

Penny   Oh, *now* we're getting to it. Come on, Bernie, five grown women still living at home. This is the time you could start to let them go.

Bernie   I'm not keeping them.

Penny   Aye. You are.

Bernie   Have you been reading those self-help books again, Penny?

Penny   You know I'm talking sense.

Bernie   'How to heal your own empty wee life.' £16.99 and a free bookmark. Where's you get the cash for crap like that Penny, do you remember? Are you going to do your job or are you going to aggravate me into a grave next to Tony? I'm fucking bereaved here, Penny!

The doorbell goes.

Bernie (*shouting at ceiling*)   Girls, you stay in your rooms! Stay inside. (*To* **Penny**.) Club's still closed, Penny, so why should I pay your wage? Make yoursel useful for once.

Penny *hesitates, then looks round the edge of the curtains.*

Penny   It's the polis again . . .

Bernie   I don't want to . . .

Penny   The lassie's opened to them.

Bernie   Is no one in this place listening to me!

A murmur of voices off. The **Careworker** *comes in, looking scared.*

Careworker   Mrs Alba? They want you to come down the station for questioning. They've got a warrant, Mrs Alba.

Bernie *wobbles for a minute, then she rallies.*

Bernie   The day of the funeral . . . Do they think they'll get to see me cry at last? Bastards. (*To the* **Careworker**.) Keep my mother in her room. Don't let her near the windows. (*To* **Penny**.) And you – get all Tony's stuff out the bedroom. I want it all gone by the time I get back. Sling it in binbags.

Penny   Bernie, just hold off on that, eh? It's too soon . . .

Bernie (*cutting her off*)   I don't even want to see a fucking Kleenex with his spit on it!

She exits. **Penny** *and the* **Careworker** *look at each other for a moment, then they follow.*

Scene Two

Bernie's *front room. Later.*

Marty *is watching the television.* **Melly** *enters and watches her for a moment.*

Melly   Did you take your pills?

Marty   For all the good they'll do me.

Melly   But you took them?

Marty   I've no faith in things, but I do them anyway. Like a machine.

Melly   You've been happier with that new doctor though, eh?

Marty (*bored*)   Have I?

Melly *is playing with her hair, trying out different looks in front of the mirror.*

Melly   Liddy didn't come to the funeral. Did you notice?

Marty   I knew she wouldn't. That new man she's got won't let her put her face round the door. When you think what a laugh she used to be . . . She doesn't even put on lippy now.

Melly   Do you think that was it? Her new man?

Marty   Who cares?

Melly   I suppose folk are still going to talk about her right enough.

Marty   Course they're going to talk. Do you think she was going to put on black and come to the funeral and look Mum in the eye? Mum would just have had to flick her one look and she'd've wet hersel.

Melly   But she never went near Dad after . . .

Marty   No, no, she'd taken up with, em . . . what's 'is name? The one whose wife topped hersel with tamazapan and tequila.

Melly   Does that kill you?

Marty   It does if you knock back a couple of bottles and take a kip in the fast lane of the M8. He drove her crazy anyway.

Melly   How?

Marty   How what?

Melly   How can a guy drive you that crazy?

Marty   You serious? I don't know. Maybe she was crazy anyway.

Melly *moves on to playing with* **Marty**'s *hair.* **Marty** *suffers it.*

Melly   Well, Liddy's well out of that.

Marty   Have you seen her new one? (*Sucks in her breath.*)
Shocking. Still – (*Laughs.*) Seems to think he can make an
honest woman out of her. Aye, good luck with that.

Melly   God, it's no wonder I can't be arsed any more. I mean,
you look at the guys out there . . .

Marty   I'm done with it. I'm telling you. I don't even want
to know. You know that thing they do in some of those African
countries, what is it, eh . . . clitorectomy? You know, when
they cut it all out and sew you up? Tell you, I'm no sure that's
not a good idea. I'm no sure that wouldn't have saved me half
the grief I've ever known.

Melly   Aw, come on, Marty!

Marty   What? I'm serious.

Melly   You had some good times with Eric. He loved you.

Marty   Oh yeah, Eric.

It was all talk with Eric, he was *weak*. See him now with that
pie-faced catering student with scone-making hands and child
bearing hips? That's what he always wanted.

Melly   He wanted you.

Marty   Did he fuck.

Melly   He did. It was just Mum made him feel such a clown.

Marty   He was a clown. He couldn't handle any of this,
could he? I tell you what they want at the end of the day
Melly, they want whatever gives them the least trouble. They
want their hole with no angst. 'Just the orifice thanks, darlin',
no personality if you don't mind, canny handle that.'

Melly (*laughing*)   Marty, that's no fair.

Maggie *enters.*

Maggie   What are you two up to?

Marty (*indicating the TV*)   What does it look like?

Melly   How about you?

Maggie   Just sorting through the last of Dad's stuff. Just for something to do. I don't want to chuck these.

She shows them. **Melly** *looks.*

Marty   What is it?

Melly   It's the holiday videos. Costa Blanca '92 and '93.

Marty   Dad was in . . . (*Stops herself.*) He wasn't even there.

Maggie   No, these were in a box at the back of the wardrobe.

Marty   We don't even have a player any more, do we?

Maggie   There's that wee telly in Nan's room.

They were good holidays. Do you remember, Melly? We just lived in that pool. Remember those jelly shoes we had?

Marty   Nan still knew seagulls from Sundays then.

Maggie   And that family next door – that boy with the dreads who took us all on his bike.

Melly   Adie bobbing about in the pool like a wee pink seal stuck in a rubber ring.

Maggie   Eating those wee sugar doughnuts and sleeping outside . . . And then we couldn't go back to that house. And we couldn't know why. We got that Dubai trip and that time in Hong Kong and it cost a bomb and it was purgatory. You've seen one Holiday Inn you've seen them all. No one knew who we were in Spain. No one. We were just a bunch of girls on holiday, having a laugh.

Marty   Didn't know what was going to hit us.

Melly   Maggie, your shoelaces's undone there.

Maggie   So?

Melly   So you'll trip over it and break your neck.

Maggie   Oh, like you'd miss me.

Marty   Where's Adie?

Maggie   Outside.

Marty   Has Mother seen her?

Maggie   She's squeezed herself into that green dress – you know, that one I found in Debenhams, of all places? This year's colour. I told you all. Adie looks a picture in it, sitting on the back step, singing.

Melly   Singing?

Maggie   Sitting there with her headphones in her ears. Wriggling her cleavage and crossing and uncrossing her legs like she's no clue some guy from the *Daily Mail* is taking twenty shots every ten seconds. It's her own little *X Factor* moment.

Melly   Mother will kill her with a blunt spoon.

Maggie   Poor wee scrap. She's too young for all this. She's still full of daydreams. I'd just like to see her happy.

Agnes *comes in waving her mobile.*

Agnes   Have you got a signal?

Maggie   Yeah, why?

Agnes   And what time do you make it?

Melly   It's just gone twelve.

Marty   Are you waiting on a call, Agnes?

Agnes *doesn't answer. She makes a disgusted noise and exits again.*
Melly *and* **Marty** *exchange a look.*

Maggie   Oh, so you know too?

Melly   Know what?

Maggie   Oh, come on!

Marty   Not following you, Maggie.

Maggie   You two know more than I do. The pair of you have always got your heads together like two little kittens chewing on one wee mouse and no one else can even get the tail. About Peter Romanov!

Marty   Oh, *him*.

Maggie (*imitating*)   'Oh, *him*.' Yeah, looks like there'll be a wee business merger going on with him and Agnes. He was out there with his dad's crowd last night. Just walking round with the dogs. You know he never normally goes on the street. And Agnes's had about twenty text messages today already.

Marty   Well, good on her. He's the best of all of them. You wouldn't even know he was a Romanov. He's so quiet and kind, he really listens when you talk to him, like he cares, you know. And he's fit.

Melly   He was the one they sent away to college, wasn't he? To be a real person. He's the suit and the business degree. He's a good match for Agnes. Good on her.

Maggie   Oh, you are so not pleased for Agnes. That is just killing the pair of you.

Marty   Maggie! You bitch!

Maggie   Like he really fancies Agnes! You know what? I wouldn't grudge her if he had fallen for her, but we all know what this is about. The Romanovs want Dad's business and this is the easy way. I know she's my sister, but come on, we're all family here. We can tell it like it is. She's pushing forty, she's got a womb full of fibroids and she looks like a stick in a skirt.

Marty   So she just got lucky.

Melly   No, Maggie's right. You know she is. This is all business. Agnes has the business. She's the businesswoman in this house, eh? Oh aye. So, Tony's gone and Agnes is the woman to know. (*Muttering*) It's fucking medieval, that's what it is.

Maggie   He's only twenty-five. He's hot. I could see it if he came sniffing round you, Melly, or even wee Adie for all she's still in school uniform. But to go poking around the house dragging out some old leftover with a face that's all nose and hairy ankles . . .

Marty   And how do you know that's not Petey's dream shag?

Maggie   Yeah, yeah.

Marty   Maybe I'm serious!

Adie *enters.*

Maggie   So? You got your agent all lined up, have you?

Adie   Have I missed anything?

Melly   If Mother sees you she'll tear your hair out.

Adie   This is my dream dress.

Marty   Yeah, you were right, Maggie. That dress works.

Adie   It works on me.

Maggie   You can keep it. I don't mind.

Adie (*kissing* **Maggie**)   Oh, it's brilliant, Maggie. Oh, this is killing me. I could've worn this to the talent show. Everyone would have seen me.

Maggie   Did they see you out there?

Adie   I made sure they saw me.

She makes the sound of clicking cameras, striking poses and laughing at them. She sings a love song, the same one she'll play throughout. She's half sending it up, half really meaning it.

Marty   If that's in the papers tomorrow, you're dead.

Maggie   The papers'll be full of Agnes and Peter Romanov.

Adie   Why?

Melly   No one's told you.

Adie   Told me what?

Maggie   It's just a wee merger.

Adie   What are you *talking* about?

Maggie   It's nothing, pet. Just . . . business.

Marty   Yeah. That's the word for it.

Pause.

Adie   That's not possible.

Maggie   It's just about the money.

Adie   She's been staring at him. She's been watching him. Does she actually think . . .

Maggie   It's business, Adie.

Pause.

Marty   What are you thinking, Adie?

Adie   I'm thinking if you don't get out of here now you'll die on that fucking couch. You better move now, Marty. Now, today, Dad's gone, Mum's no looking, last chance. Shift yourself now or you'll never do it. *We're all going to die in this house!*

Maggie   Adie! God's sake, calm down!

Adie   I'm serious. I can't do it. I'm not stopping here with all of you, five battery hens in one cage pecking each other's feathers out till you're all old and bald and ugly. I'm not stopping here like a bit of Mum's china gathering dust. I'm breaking out. I'm going up town in this dress, tonight. I'm leaving. I'm fucking emigrating!

Marty   Oh shut up, will you!

Adie *breaks down in noisy tears. The* **Careworker** *enters. She hesitates but as no one else moves she goes to hold* **Adie***.*

Careworker   He wouldn't want you to grieve like this pet. He wouldn't.

Adie *gets her tears under control. The doorbell goes. No one moves. The* **Careworker** *looks round at them all.*

Careworker   I am no your servant, ladies.

No one moves. The doorbell goes again.

Could be anyone. Could be important.

Still nothing. The bell goes again.

(*Going for door.*)   I am not paid for this, I am not.

She exits.

Marty   You think you're the only person that's ever felt like that, don't you, Adie?

Maggie   You better change back, Adie.

The **Careworker** *comes back in with a huge bouquet of red flowers.*

Careworker   You see the size of that car out there?

Melly   Yes.

Careworker   Revs like a bull gargling thunder.

Maggie   Peter Romanov himself, was it?

Careworker   I don't know. Condolences, I suppose. Why didn't they send them to the church?

Marty   Because these are for us.

She helps herself to a flower and exits.

Maggie (*looking at card*)   They're for Agnes?

Melly   Who cares? I deserve flowers and I don't get them.

She helps herself and follows **Marty**. **Maggie** *hesitates, then takes a few blooms and follows.*

Careworker (*to* **Adie**)   All right, pet?

Adie *says nothing, just looking at the flowers. The careworker exits.* **Adie** *helps herself to one rose and holds it to her face. She exits.*

Bernie *and* **Penny** *enter.* **Bernie** *is very tense.*

Bernie   What was he playing at? What did he think he was *playing* at?

Penny   Everything's in Agnes's name? All the companies? Everything?

Bernie   Everything that's visible.

Penny   You thought there'd be a bit for you, didn't you? Or at least for the girls. Well, the companies don't really make any money, do they? You've still got the real money. What's the problem?

Bernie   Are you still here? Club's not opening today, get off home.

Penny   I'm here on my own time today. As a friend.

Agnes *comes through. She's finishing a call.*

Agnes   All right . . . we'll set up a meeting for next week. Thanks. Yes. Bye.

Bernie *stares at her for a moment.*

Bernie   Business as usual, is it? We buried your father today.

Agnes   He wasn't my father.

Bernie   He saw you right though, didn't he? He left it all to you and you don't have the sense to know you're paddling with piranhas.

Agnes   Well, we'll see what I know, won't we?

Bernie   Oh, *you're* sorting us out, are you? Oh well, we're laughing, aren't we? Aren't you just the image of your Auntie Ida that worked in the bank? Get your calculator out, Agnes. Tell us your big plan, eh?

Agnes   It's just a question of . . .

Bernie   What?

Agnes   We need to consolidate the floating assets into property and −

Bernie   Aw, the *floating* assets? You going to pull them into the bank and pick them up by the hair and look in their wet wee faces and ask them how the repayments are coming along?

Agnes   I don't . . .

Bernie   Or shall I talk to Daddy Romanov about that bit of the *business*? Was that him on the phone?

Agnes   It was Peter.

Bernie   Well, shall we ring Daddy Romanov and tell him you're handling everything now? That what you want, darling?

Agnes   I just think . . .

Bernie *grabs her face.*

Bernie   Well, don't think, pet, don't think. 'Cause I reckon there's some things you don't want to think about. This family's fortune is lying out on the road where Tony dropped it and we only get to pick it up now if the big boys say we can. You can have your name on all the bank statements you like but if you want Mummy to keep the big bad wolf from eating you from the toes up you better give me some respect. Hear me?

Agnes   Let me go!

Bernie *pushes her away.*

Bernie   You can go, but you'll go where I tell you, hear me?

Agnes *is crying.*

Penny   Christ, Bernie . . .

Bernie   *What?!*

Pause.

Penny   What do you want me to do with the rest of Tony's things?

Bernie   I told you. Bin the lot of –

Penny *interrupts her by taking a gun out of her bag and holding it up.*

Penny   I couldn't just put it in the rubbish, Bernie.

Bernie *hesitates.*

Bernie   Put it in the safe.

There's a concealed safe in the room. **Penny** *opens it and puts the gun away.*

The other daughters enter.

Maggie What's going on?

Bernie Nothing's going on.

Penny *exits.*

Maggie (*to* **Agnes**) What's she crying for? She's the only one that's got a chance now, isn't she?

Agnes You keep your tongue in its hole!

Bernie You can all keep quiet! The only thing keeping the sky from dropping on your stupid heads is me! And I'll do it till they put me in a box, but you will do what I tell you!

An argument off. The **Careworker** *and* **Mary**. **Mary** *bursts in with the* **Careworker** *on her heels.* **Mary** *is wearing sixties finery, earrings and heavy make-up.*

Mary Bernadette, where's my blue scarf? I don't want this lot getting hold of it. They're not getting any of it. Not my earrings, not my dancing shoes. None of them will ever be loved. None of them. They've got hearts like raisins. Bernadette, give me my pearl earrings!

Bernie (*to* **Careworker**) Will you get her out of here?

The **Careworker** *is buttoning her coat.*

Careworker My shift finished an hour ago, Mrs Alba.

Mary I'm running away. I'm in love. He loves me. We'll walk into the sea together. We'll lie on the sand and a wave will rush over us like that film . . . what was that film, Bernadette? None of these could love a man, they've got plastic heads like dolls with nothing inside. No real man would love them. Men that screw plastic dolls, that's all they're fit for.

Bernie Mother, shut up!

Mary   I won't shut up! I'm not stopping here with these dead bits of plastic. Nothing in their eyes but malice and disgust. I want to go home, Bernie. I want to lie on the beach and open my legs to the waves.

Bernie (*shouting to* **Careworker**)   Get her out of here!

Mary *starts banging on the window. The* **Careworker** *just exits.* **Bernie** *grabs* **Mary***'s wrist.*

Mary   Let go of me, Bernadette!

Bernie   Help me, will you?!

They all take hold of **Mary**.

Mary   Let me out, Bernadette! I want to go to the sea. I love him. He's waiting by the sea. I love him! Let me go!

Scene Three

The front room of **Bernie***'s house. A few days later.*

All the young women apart from **Adie** *are busy emptying and sorting boxes of paperwork and computer disks.*

Penny *is with them.*

They are all weary and deeply unenthusiastic about the task, apart from **Agnes**.

Adie*'s love theme is faint upstairs. It is raining heavily and relentlessly. The rain continues until nearly the end of the play now.*

Agnes (*pushing one box aside*)   That's all receipts.

Marty (*busy with calculator*)   Give it to Melly.

Maggie (*sarcastic*)   Is Peter coming over later to help you 'audit the accounts', Agnes?

Agnes   No.

Upstairs **Adie***'s music has finished.*

Maggie (*calling upstairs*) Adie! Adie, get down here!

The same song starts again from the beginning.

Melly She'll be lying in her bed.

Penny There's something up with that girl. She can't keep still, she's shaking all over like she's got a temperature or a daddy-long-legs between her tits.

Marty Yeah, well, we're all sick here, Penny.

Maggie Except Agnes.

Agnes That's right. I'm feeling great. If you don't like it, you can eat it.

Maggie See, I always thought it was your looks that were your best feature, Agnes, but, you know, your manners are right up there, eh?

Agnes Christ, I can't wait to get shot of the lot of you.

Maggie Oh, how's that going to work? You going to put us on the street? You think Mum'll stand for that?

Marty Change the record, will you!

Agnes You've woken up now, haven't you? Big ugly Agnes with her head full of numbers, let's all rip the piss out of her because she canny walk in heels. Well, Melly's got knock-off Manolos, you've got a Magimix but I've got a life.

Maggie Yeah, yeah.

Melly Aw, the sound of that rain is cracking my heid open! Draw the curtains, Penny, I canny stand to look out.

Penny *draws the curtains.*

Marty I couldn't sleep last night for the rain on the roof.

Melly Neither could I.

Maggie I got up to get something to warm me. The rain died down for a moment. There was this tiny window in the clouds and the moon looked out. Then it was just dark again.

Penny   The gutters were running when I was letting the strippers in. The rain was washing the muck in the door. That was about one, when Peter Romanov was dropping you off round the side, Agnes.

Maggie   God, that *late*? Oh, you're such a party animal, Agnes. What time did he leave?

Agnes   What do you care?

Melly   Must have been about half one.

Agnes   How do you know?

Melly   I heard his car.

Penny   But I saw it still out there at four when I was locking up.

Agnes   It can't have been him.

Penny   You can't mistake that car.

Marty   I heard it revving after four.

Maggie   Well, how weird is that?

Pause.

Penny   So, Agnes, are we going to need our wedding hats?

The other women look at each other.

Agnes   Oh, I don't know. It's early days.

Marty   It's so strange, isn't it? In the midst of grief you just turn towards life, don't you? You think that's what's going on, Agnes? True love born out of trauma, eh?

Agnes   I'm not saying I'm in love.

Melly   Well, I'd have him.

Agnes   There's a lot to talk about. He helps his father like I helped Tony. We see what needs to be done for our families. That's all.

Marty   So you've not snogged him then?

Agnes   Well, of course, but that's not the point, is it?!

Melly   Agnes, have you even shagged him?

Agnes   We get on fine, all right? Is that so surprising?

Melly   Agnes, honey, we're really not getting at you, we just want to know what he was like.

Agnes   Fine. Everything works. What do you want to know?

Penny   Oh darlin', just that you're happy.

Agnes   Of course I am. He's very . . . considerate.

Marty   That's it?

Agnes   Marty, I was choking on my own heart. It's all still just . . . awkward. Is that what you want to hear? I'm being honest. We've got to get to know each other. It's never easy, is it?

Maggie   I don't think I'd have any problem shagging Peter Romanov.

Agnes   Well, you'll never know, will you, Maggie?

Penny   The thing is, Agnes, the Romanovs have had it tough. His dad and him have had to pull themselves up from nothing. Men like that can't go letting their feelings spill out so easy. Now see, the first time my man Colin and me got it together – oh wow . . .

She starts to laugh.

Melly   What happened?

Penny   Well, we were so young, really. I used to hang out where he was playing football after school, you know, *staring* at him from the side of the field, thinking he's got to get the message. Shorter and shorter skirts, I'd chilblains on my knees and I was getting a terrible reputation, but he never twigged. In the end I had to grab him by the ears and drag him behind the lavvy at the top of the park. Oh, he got the idea then, oh my God, it was like a tornado on viagra, but after, I kid you not, he just wept. He did. He held on to me and he wept, and he's telling me I'm the most beautiful thing in the world, and he's patting the ground, all needles and cans and used condoms and he says, 'This is a sacred place for me now.' Can you believe it?

Maggie   Oh, that is so *sweet*!

Melly (*listening*)   Is that Mum back?

They all listen.

Maggie   No, we're all right.

Melly   Aw, will you look! (*Shows them nails.*) And I won't get out to get them fixed, will I? (*Pushes box aside.*) I don't want to do this any more.

Marty   So are you saying he was your *only* man, ever?

Penny   Oh no, listen, I bloomed early. I was his though. I'm sure of that. He had me and he had his canaries and that was all he wanted till the day he died, bless him. You girls should listen to this. It's easy enough to get yoursel something hot on a Saturday night but if you want to be warm your whole life you need to love people for who they are.

Melly   You loved him all those years, Penny?

Penny   I love him yet. That's a real thing.

Marty   I heard you used to hit him.

Penny   Well, I'm no saying I was anyone's doormat! Aye, I nearly put his eye out once.

Maggie   Aw, that's more like it!

Penny   See, your Mum and me are out the same mould. God forgive me, I killed his canaries once, with a rolling pin. I don't know what he said to me to spark that off. Oh, I'm bad sometimes. But he forgave me.

They're all laughing. **Adie***'s music has stopped.*

Melly   Agnes, we can't make sense of any of this, no one could. I've had it.

Agnes   Leave it then. You're only making a worse mess. I can sort all of this faster on my own.

She starts gathering up the paperwork.

Marty (*dropping calculator*)   Thank you.

Maggie (*calling upstairs*)   Adie? Come on down, we're finished!

Melly   Adie?

No sound or music upstairs.

Maggie (*getting up*)   I'll go and see what she's up to.

Penny   That girl is ill.

Marty   Of course she is, she hardly sleeps.

Penny   So what does she do?

Marty   How would I know?

Penny   So how do you know she's no sleeping?

Agnes   She's got a thing about Peter. It's killing her I'm with him.

Melly   How do you make that out?

Agnes   Look at her face next time we're together. She looks like she's going to have a breakdown on the spot.

Marty   You know, you're so smug that you're the only one in the family that's never needed Prozac, it doesny mean you're sane, Agnes, it just means you don't have any imagination.

Maggie *and* **Adie** *enter.*

Maggie   Here's Sleeping Beauty. Not sleeping, apparently.

Adie   I'm sick.

Marty   Didn't you sleep well last night then?

Adie   Yes.

Marty   So what's the problem?

Adie Leave me alone! Why do you care if I'm sleeping?!

Marty I'm just worried about you!

Adie Just nosy, more like it! I thought you were supposed to have your head in a box of papers looking for Agnes's fortune! You found it yet? No? Well, why don't you get back in your box, Marty? God, I wish I was invisible so I could get through this place without everyone asking me where I'm going!

The **Careworker** *comes in.*

Careworker There's some guy downstairs with a delivery. Your mother says you've all got to come and help.

No one moves.

Careworker Listen, it's no even my job to give you messages, there's no way I'm humping boxes.

They all drift out apart from **Adie** *and* **Penny**. **Marty** *gives* **Adie** *a look as she passes.*

Adie What's the matter? You trying to work out what normal looks like? (*She points to her own face.*) Here you go. Take a good look. Now run off and play with razor blades again.

Marty *leaves.*

Penny She's your sister, Adie – that was cruel.

Adie She follows me everywhere. Sometimes she creeps into my room to see if I'm sleeping. And all the time she's going, 'Oh Adie, it's such a shame, all that hope in you and it's just going to be flattened. God, I remember being where you are and it just comes to fag ends and broken glass.' It doesn't! I won't! I'm not like her!

Penny You're seeing Peter Romanov, aren't you? It's not just a crush you've got, you're –

Adie *Shut up!* (*More quietly.*) What if I am?

Penny (*dropping her voice*) My *God*, Adie, what do you think you're playing at?!

Adie   You think you know what's going on, but you haven't a clue.

Penny   Does his father know?

Adie   It's our business, no one else's.

Penny   You better change your ideas right now!

Adie   You have no idea.

Penny   I've an idea where this'll end up! I can see that plain enough!

Adie   Don't look, Penny. It'll blind you.

Penny   I could read this story with my fingertips. You're throwing yourself off the fifteenth floor and you haven't even twigged you're falling. Do you think it's *love*, Adie? You're tumbling about in the cold wind, falling with your nightie round your head and you think this is *romance*?

Adie   I think you'll never understand it, Penny.

Penny   Oh honey, there's nothing new on this earth when it comes to what men and women do in the dark. First love is when you learn. So you've learned that love can open you up like spring sun on a wee primrose. Good. Remember that. You know how to love. Well learned. But he's marrying Agnes. You know it. I know it. And you and I *and* Agnes and all know fine he doesny love her but marry her he will. So you can break your heart for the next twenty years raging and weeping and shagging him in secret at Christmas and christenings or you can take your lesson and show some other boy what you've learned. That's the way it is.

Adie   Shut up.

Penny   No, I won't shut up!

Adie   What do you care? It's none of your business.

Penny   I do care and that makes you my business! I've known you from a wee pink egg, Adie.

Adie   But you're not family! Are you?! You're just some old witch Mum pays to keep bar and wipe the floors, you drag our business out with the dust and drool over it! Go find some family of your own to chew on!

Penny   Blood's nothing to do with it. Thirty years. You're part of my life, I'm part of yours. I don't want to spend my days in a war zone.

Adie   What about Agnes? You care about her too? You going to give her your little speech about love?

Penny   If the pipe's burst you can't plug the leak. I'll not see her hurt worse though, Adie, I'm warning you.

Adie   Then you better keep quiet, hadn't you? You're too late, Penny. Do you think I care if you're clucking away behind me? You think I'm scared what my mum might do? I'm not falling, Penny, I'm flying, I'm soaring over the lot of you. What are you going to tell Mum, that I'm in love? You think she could take a belt and beat that out of me? Think you can catch me now? Where's your wings, Penny?

Penny   Adie, you are heading for a fall that'll break you in bits. And I'll shine a spotlight on the wreck if I have to!

Adie   Turn all the lights on! Crank up the music, Penny, sell tickets so the world can see what it's missing. He's mine.

Penny   You're that sure?

Adie   When I look into his eyes it's as if I'm slowly drinking his blood.

Penny   I can't listen to this.

Adie   You'll have to. I haven't been scared of making you angry since I was eight, Penny.

Agnes *enters.*

Agnes   What are you arguing about now?

Penny   She wants me to go to the corner shop in this rain, as if she didn't have two good legs of her own.

Agnes   Oh, Penny, did you bring me that catalogue?

Penny   On your bed – you won't believe the prices and they do the alterations online. My neighbour's girl looked like Kate Moss for £250. I've left you the honeymoon lingerie pull-out as well.

Agnes *exits.*

Adie   Not bursting her bubble today then?

Penny   I don't know what I'm going to do, Adie.

Marty, **Maggie** *and* **Melly** *enter.*

Maggie (*to* **Adie**)   Have you seen the boxes out there?

Melly   Net-a-Porter. Someone's been clicking her mouse.

Maggie   She has got herself such beautiful things, Adie.

Marty *holds some classy designer lingerie up against herself.*

Adie   *Agnes* bought that?

Marty   No, this is for me.

Adie   Where d'you get the money for that?

Marty   I've put everything on a new card.

Adie   Well, who's going to see you in it?

Marty   What do you care? Why? Do you want to borrow it?

Penny   It's beautiful. You don't need to be seen in something like that, makes you feel better just having it on.

Marty   I love silk on my skin, don't you? Pure cotton, linen, natural fabrics, they let you breathe. I'm going to buy everything natural from the skin out. I'm going to make myself fresh.

Penny (*looking out at boxes*)   Agnes is the one giving herself a makeover. Wouldn't that be great? Just to buy yourself a whole new look, all at once. We're not going to recognise her, girls. Before you know it she'll be in the colour supplements as a design icon.

Maggie   Or she'll pop out Romanov twins and turn back into a sack of potatoes.

Melly   Have you seen the aunts? About thirty kids each and I saw one of them breast-feeding in the street.

Penny   Well, at least that wain's getting cuddles.

Marty   You like baby sick so much, go and work for them.

Penny   My job's here. With your mother. Always will be.

Music from downstairs.

Melly   Is that the wedding reception?

Penny   They must be starting the dancing.

Maggie   It's not a wedding reception.

Adie   The two of them will be dancing together, everyone watching.

Maggie   You know what I'm saying, you can't call it a proper wedding.

Melly   If someone stuck by me for fifteen years and still wanted a slow dance I'd be happy.

Marty   Some chance.

Melly   Oh, the rain out there, the whole world's weeping.

Penny   They won't care about the weather. I've never seen anything like it. This is their day at last and they're only looking at each other. Never saw so many beautiful men in one place. There must be fifty of them down there.

Maggie   But it's not a wedding!

Penny   Well, what would you call it then? Best reception I've ever seen. Happy?! They're shaking the rafters, hear them! They know how to enjoy themselves. There's one boy there in sequins that does a turn with an accordion. I tell you, if I thought I could turn him I'd follow him about all day. The green eyes on him, tight wee body. Fifteen, twenty of them that you just want to stare at for the pleasure of it, like looking at a flower garden.

But the happy couple aren't even noticing. Jason looks like a frog in a kilt but Fraser can't see another man in the room. That's for ever.

Melly   Do you think?

Adie   Yes. Why not?

Penny   Jason's mother's down there. She threw him out in the street when he first told her what he was, and now she wouldn't settle till they promised they'd come back here for the wedding . . .

Maggie (*cutting in*)   It's not a real (wedding) . . .

Adie (*cutting in*)   Well, what is it then?

Penny   Her son's found true love, she wants the world to see. There's nothing better than real love.

Adie   No. There isn't.

Maggie   I don't think there's anything real about it.

Melly   It's like believing in Santa. I'd give anything to be able to do that again.

A love song, dance song, many voices joining in below.

Penny   They're all on the floor now. Oh, I love this one.

Adie   Makes you feel it.

The song swells below, then dies away in applause. As it ends, the sound of the rain louder. The women listen.

Melly   Even the rain's got the beat.

Marty   They're happy, aren't they?

Adie   Can we go down? Can we dance? Oh come on, I want to dance, forget everything for a while.

Marty   What have you got to forget?

Adie   I can have things on my mind too.

Marty   No kidding?

Penny   Shoosh, will you! I want to listen.

More singing below. As they listen **Adie** *starts to move to the music,* **Marty** *then* **Melly** *joins in, all of them are singing along. They crescendo and stop as the applause rings out below.*

Penny   Now they'll have the buffet. I better go lend a hand.

Adie   Why can't we go down?

Penny   Adie, you weren't invited.

Penny *exits.*

Maggie   Who'd want to be invited? And it's not a real wedding.

She exits. After a moment **Adie** *follows.* **Marty** *has slumped.* **Melly** *comes to sit by her.*

Melly   What's wrong with you?

Marty   I just want the rain to stop so I can get out.

Melly   Out where?

Marty   I don't care! Somewhere dry!

Melly   It makes the grass grow.

Marty   It makes the world rot. (*Pause.*) Were you in last night?

Melly   We're all in every night these days.

Marty   So did you hear someone else coming in about four in the morning?

Melly   Who?

Marty   I don't know. That's why I'm asking you.

Melly   Maybe it was Penny closing up the club.

Marty   It sounded like someone coming in the back door.

Melly   God, Marty, do you think it was someone thieving?

Marty (*bitter*)   Well, funny you should say that.

Melly   Have you checked the back door? Have you told Mum? We better tell Mum.

Marty   No, no, don't do that. Maybe I imagined it.

Melly   I don't think you'd imagine a thing like that.

Marty   No, just leave it.

Melly *hesitates then goes to leave.*

Marty   Melly . . .

Melly (*at the door*)   What?

Marty   Nothing.

Pause.

Melly   What's wrong, Marty?

Pause.

Marty   Nothing. I don't know what I'm saying.

Pause.

Melly   You should get some rest.

Agnes *bursts in, furious.*

Agnes   Which of you was it! Who's been trying to talk to Peter behind my back!

Marty   What are you talking about?

Agnes   He told me! One of you's been phoning him!

Melly   So ask him who it was!

Marty   Why would he tell you that?

Penny, **Maggie** *and* **Adie** *enter.*

Adie   What's going on?

Agnes Was it you? Have you been phoning Peter behind my back?

Maggie You've got a nerve, Agnes!

Agnes A voice like mine, he said! Talking all kinds of filth.

Marty Maybe he's ringing chatlines, Agnes. Maybe you just haven't got what it takes to keep a young man happy.

Agnes You take that back! One of you is trying to ruin everything.

Penny Look, calm down, Agnes, they can hear you downstairs!

Agnes I want to know who it was!

Adie If he doesn't know why should we? It could have been anyone. (*She is looking at* **Marty**.)

Marty Anyone with a phone and an itchy finger. How're your fingers, Adie?

Bernie *enters.*

Bernie The groom's mother has just come up and asked me if we could keep it down while the speeches are on.

Marty Which groom?

Bernie What is going on?

Agnes One of them has been ringing Peter in the middle of the night. Telling him they'll give him something better than I'll ever have! Telling him . . . (*She can't go on.*)

Bernie Who has?

Agnes One of them! He knew the voice!

Bernie (*very still, very angry*) Now why would anyone want to do a thing like that? (*To* **Agnes**.) He's sure?

Agnes Yes!

Bernie So I worry and I work and I put another ten lines Botox won't shift on this face to sort you out, to keep you safe, to keep you fed and shod and fat and happy, and one of you is clueless enough to go and shoogle the house of cards, are they? For what? For *laughs*? (*Pause.*) Let's see your phones.

Maggie   What for?

Bernie   Anyone stupid enough to pull a stunt like that won't have the sense to fix her phone record, will she?

She holds out her hand. **Maggie** *gives* **Bernie** *her mobile. The others are already looking for theirs, all except* **Marty**. **Bernie** *passes the phones to* **Agnes**, *who checks the numbers and tosses them back.* **Bernie** *is nose to nose with* **Marty**.

Marty   I've lost it. I tried ringing it, but the battery's dead.

Penny (*looking*)   It's down the seat cushion there.

She picks it out, looks.

The battery's fine.

She passes it to **Agnes**. **Agnes** *checks the phone. She catches her breath, she looks up at* **Marty**, *accusation all over her face.*

Bernie   You!

She moves in on **Marty**, *who grabs up something to defend herself.*

Marty   Don't you hit me!

Bernie   I'll hit you if I want to!

Marty   If I let you! Do you hear me?! Get away from me!

Penny   Marty, put that down!

Agnes *grabs* **Bernie** *back.*

Agnes   Stop it! Mum, please!

Bernie   Look at her! Look at the face on her! She's laughing at us!

Marty   You'd laugh if you could see the state of yourself.

Bernie   We could lose *everything*! What were you doing?!

Marty (*quietly*)   It was just a joke.

Adie   Since when have you fancied yourself a comedian, Marty? You're nearly bursting with everything bottled up in there. Why don't you just tell us?

Marty   You want me to tell you? You sure? If I told just half the truth that's in me this place would burst into flames.

Adie   There's no truth in you, Marty, just acid and disappointment.

Bernie   Adie, be quiet!

Maggie   Why are you two going at each other? You're both mad.

Melly   Why do you have to smash everything, Marty?

Marty   Oh, you think it's me doing that?

Adie   Bring it on, Marty. Light your fire. Let's see who's burning if you throw that match.

Bernie   Adie, are you in this too? I'll finish you!

Agnes   She's got a crush on Peter. She can't bear knowing we're together.

Adie   You're not together! You're in business!

Agnes   Mum, tell her!

Bernie   Adie, button it!

Melly   It was you told us it was business!

Maggie   You did, you said you both knew how to arrange things for the family.

Bernie   Be quiet! All of you! I knew you'd bring these walls down round my ears, but I thought you'd let me get the grave dirt out from under my fingernails first. Look at you all, pouring your hate on my head like hailstones. But I'm not old yet. You won't finish me. I'll give you what's best for you if I have to beat it into you. My God, if you'd had the life I've had you might be fit for me. Now take your fat, marshmallow faces and your soggy tears away to your rooms and give me peace!

They all exit except **Penny**. **Bernie** *is pacing.*

Bernie   It's not broken. Nothing's spoiled. I can fix this.

Penny   Can I say something?

Bernie   Can I stop you? Christ, you saw all of that, didn't you? Who am I kidding – you see everything anyway.

Penny   I keep your business to myself, Bernie. You know that.

Bernie   We need to bring the wedding forward.

Penny   You think Agnes'll get cold feet after this?

Bernie   Not her! Him!

Penny   Well, I don't see that, Bernie, if he hadn't told her about the calls mebbe, but –

Bernie   How does it look? We're offering a partnership in good faith and one of our own is sneaking around trying to poison the wedding cake. We need to get a date. Everyone needs to see this go through. So we all feel secure.

Penny   I see what you're saying. Aye, good thinking.

Bernie   I don't *think*, Penny. I don't waste my time. I see what needs doing and I see it gets done.

Penny   And you think Peter might be having second thoughts?

Bernie   What are you driving at, Penny?

Penny   Well . . . of course his family know how neat it'll all be if he marries Agnes.

Bernie   So where's the problem? Out with it. I can see you've a knife ready there.

Penny   I'm not trying to knife you, Bernie, it's just a wee thought I had.

Bernie   About what?

Penny   Look, if you don't want to know that suits me. If you do, keep your eyes open and you'll see what I'm saying quick enough. Like a paving slab in your face.

Bernie   What'll I see?

Penny   I thought you were the clever one? I thought you were the one that could read folk's thoughts just by sniffing the air they'd breathed. When it comes to your own, you're as blind as the rest of us, aren't you?

Bernie   Are we talking about Marty?

Penny   Aye, fine, let's start with Marty. Why would she phone Peter like that ?

Bernie   You heard her. She thinks she's funny.

Penny   Oh, and you believed that?

Bernie   That's what she's like, Penny! Twisted.

Penny   Fine. So if you heard the same story about your neighbours over the road there, what would you think then?

Bernie   Oh, I can see the point of that knife now.

Penny   Bernie, I'm trying to help you. I know it's not been easy for you, but you can't take it out on the girls. They'd be better off out of all of this but you won't let them go. That's why they're twisted! Why didn't you let Agnes stay married? Why didn't you let Marty make her own life away from here?

Bernie   Me? I never stopped them!

Penny   You did! You nipped at them and tore at them, told Agnes her man was a sheep with no teeth, told Marty she was fit for nothing but tears and tantrums and never would be. You took all the rage and disappointment Tony'd put in your heart and let it flow all over them like lava. Till they were nothing but dust. Till you could sweep them up and carry them back home where you wanted them. You do it to all of them.

Bernie   You're talking crap, Penny.

Penny   All right. Let it all go. Let Tony's money vanish into the court's accounting book. Let the girls out this cage. Who are you then, Bernie?

Bernie   A better woman than you, Penny Robertson.

Penny   A richer one mebbe. (*Checks herself.*) Bernie, you've never seen me without a wage. I'm not forgetting that. I never will.

Bernie   You call this gratitude?

Penny   Marty just needs to sort herself out. But there's more than that, Bernie, that's what I'm telling you . . .

Bernie (*cutting her off*)   You know what I think? I think you're making up mysteries to feel a wee bit important. I think your shabby sad sack of a life is so empty you have to come here and fill your greedy soul with bits of mine. Well, let me tell you, what happens to my daughters is my business and I know my own business!

Penny   And I think you're making your bed on a volcano. You could lose it all, Bernie.

Bernie   Oh, you'd like that, wouldn't you? To see me and the girls out on the street?

Penny   No. But that doesn't mean it won't happen!

Bernie   No, Penny, there's only one person here couldn't drag herself off the street without coming crying to her pals, and any time you fancy earning your rent in doorways again you let me know. It's what your mummy taught you, after all.

Penny   You leave my mother out of this!

Bernie   Then you keep your fat beak out of my family!

Penny   Fine. I tried to tell you. I tried to be a friend to you.

Bernie (*cutting in*)   I pay you to do fuck-all and you don't even do that! You hang around up here, wittering on and on.

Penny (*cutting in*)   Look, Bernie, what about Adie?

Bernie   What about Adie? She's back at school next week.

Penny   It's real, you know. She's crazy about Peter Romanov.

Bernie   Poor wee Adie. It'll be a learning experience won't it?

She smiles as she sees **Penny***'s surprise.*

Bernie   Oh what? You thought I didn't know?

Penny   You know what they've been up to? Because put aside the fact that's she's barely old enough for him, I think that's a bit of a time bomb to chuck in Agnes's marriage bed, don't you?

Bernie   They're not *up* to anything outside Adie's fevered wee brain! You think I'd let her near a wolf like a Romanov? You think I'm stupid? You're just trying to give me bad dreams, Penny. I'm not listening to any more of this, because if I do I'll rip you open.

Penny   You don't scare me, Bernie.

Bernie (*cutting in*)   My daughters know when they're well off. They know they can never cross me! Never!

Penny   Oh aye. You've got a good grip on their wee wings, but you loosen your fingers, even for one second, and they'll be off over the rooftops.

Bernie   And I've got stones ready to bring them down. They need me. They need to be here. That's it.

Penny   You're a woman that knows what she wants, Bernie.

Bernie   And I'm not afraid to get it.

Penny   And you're right. Peter Romanov can't have time for anyone but Agnes, and she's just as keen. Steamy windows at her age. Who'd've thought it, eh? I wouldn't have believed it myself if I hadn't seen his car still out there at four thirty this morning when I was closing up.

Agnes *comes in at the end of this.*

Bernie   At four thirty?

Agnes   Peter dropped me off at one.

Bernie   Are you sure?

Marty *is on.*

Agnes   Of course I'm sure. He's never dropped me back later than one.

Marty   Well, I heard his car out there after four.

Bernie   How do you know? Did you see him?

Marty   I wasn't going to lean out the window, was I? But you can't mistake the noise that car makes. (*To* **Agnes**.) You came in the back door last night, didn't you?

Agnes   Why would I come in the back door!

Adie is on. There is banging, then rowdy shouting starting below.

Bernie   What's going on here?!

Penny   Och, you'll soon work it out, Bernie. You know everything that's going on round here. So I saw Peter's car parked up and shaking at four in the morning right by your back gate. Tell me what that means, Bernie?

Bernie   You got the time wrong.

Penny   You believe that, Bernie. If it makes you feel better.

Adie   Mum, she's just stirring it.

Long pause. **Bernie** *just stares at* **Adie**.

Bernie   Oh, I know she is. There's mongrel dogs all round us trying to paw their dirt on to us – well, they'll get a brick on their sniffing noses if they try it!

Marty   So what's going on?

Penny   Because you know something is.

Bernie   Nothing. (*Staring at* **Adie**.) Nothing, because I just put a stop to it *right now*! I was born with my eyes wide open and I can keep them open and never blink till they bury me. Hear me?

Agnes   I have a right to know what's going on!

Bernie   You don't have any rights except to do what I tell you. I made you, I'm in the bones of you. If you imagine you've got one thought that's your own you're kidding yourself. That's it. (*To* **Penny**.) And you mind your own business and keep your mouth shut.

The noise below surges, violence, screaming. The **Careworker** *comes in.*

Careworker   I think someone should call the police. There's . . . I think something's happening in the club.

Bernie (*to* **Penny**)   Get down there and see what's happening.

Penny *leaves. The* **Careworker** *follows. The noise surges.* **Bernie** *snatches up her baseball bat and exits.*

The young women look at each other in silence, then first **Agnes***, then* **Melly** *and* **Maggie** *exit too.*

There is distant screaming and crying downstairs.

Marty   You can't say I dropped you in it.

Adie   You actually do want him, don't you?

Marty   Give me a break.

Adie   You do. A fresh start, clean and new and natural. You're too dirty for him, Marty. Shop-soiled.

Marty   You're lying to yourself, Adie.

Adie   You want him, but I love him. I *love* him, Marty. I know how to do that.

Marty   He listened to me, Adie, he took the calls, he *listened*. I could hear him breathing.

Adie   We *both* listened, Marty. Together. I cried for you. (*Pause.*) He's going to take me away.

Marty   He's taking you in the back seat of his car, Adie! What does that tell you?

Adie   That there's nowhere on earth we can't be happy if we're touching each other.

Marty   I'm not letting it happen, Adie.

The noise surges again below. **Maggie**, **Agnes** *and* **Melly** *enter.*

Maggie   God, it's bad.

Penny *and* **Bernie** *are back in,* **Penny** *agitated,* **Bernie** *impassive.*

Penny   Police are coming.

Adie   What's happening?

Penny   Gatecrashers.

Bernie   Queer-bashers.

Adie   What?

Bernie   Some idiot let them in.

Penny   They couldn't get the door barred, there's no
doormen working an afternoon wedding! They just piled in.
(*Going to window.*) Oh God, where are the police? Bernie,
Bernie, they've got Fraser! They've got him in the car park!
(*Hammering on window.*) Leave him, leave him, you animals! The
police are coming! I know you! I'll know you!

Bernie (*pulling her*)   Get away from the windows before they
put a brick through them!

Penny   Oh Mother of God, help him! His face, Bernie!
They're killing him.

Marty   That'll be the death of true love then.

Adie   No! Mum! Stop them! We have to stop them!

Adie *runs for the door.* **Bernie** *grabs her.*

Bernie   There's no stopping them, pet, so you stay here
with me. They were asking for it anyway. Putting on a wedding
reception? In this place? I was mad to take the booking.
They're no getting their deposit back, that's for sure, every
glass in the place broken.

Noise of the fight outside.

Penny (*looking round edge of window*)   Oh, finish it, please just
stop . . .

Distant sirens.

Bernie   That'll shift them.

Penny   Oh, look at him! Oh, Jason's trying to lift him. His head's broken, Bernie.

Bernie   And him just married.

Marty   Well, what do you think, Mum, do you think young love lasts when it's had its looks kicked to bits?

Bernie   I think life gets you that way sooner or later and hell mend you if you're fool enough to think different.

Adie (*screaming at them*)   What are you talking about! The two of you sitting there *talking*! How can you . . . ?!

Bernie (*erupting, shouting her down*)   The wee poof's getting what he deserves! Break his stupid head open and kick some sense into it! (*Shouting right at* **Adie**.) And you sit in your place and keep quiet from now on! Hear me?! You hearing me Adie?!

Sirens getting closer, police and ambulance.

Fade lights.

Scene Four

Upstairs, night. Thumping music and pub noise coming up from downstairs.

The young women are sharing a take-out, squabbling half-heartedly over the remote. **Marty** *wins and sits channel-hopping.*

Bernie *is drinking, staring at the screen without seeing it.*

Prue, *sixty-something, Tony's cousin and an old neighbour, sits watching* **Bernie** *nervously.* **Prue** *is poised for flight.*

Prue   Well . . . I won't keep you . . . (*She half rises.*)

Bernie   What's your hurry? We hardly see you these days, anyway.

Prue   I don't think that cab's coming, Bernie. I'll miss the last bus.

Bernie   They're our cabs, Prue – he'll be here, sit down.

Prue *sits down.*

Bernie   How's that man of yours?

Prue   Just the same.

Bernie   We never see him either.

Prue   Well, you know what he's like. I mean, we were both sorry not to make the funeral. He just . . . he doesn't go out, you know? He's on invalidity. I think it's depression myself but you can't tell him.

Bernie   Never could tell him. How's he getting on with your daughter?

Prue   He won't forgive her.

Bernie   Good on him.

Prue   Well, it's breaking my heart, Bernie, that's the truth of it.

Bernie   She turned her back on you, Prue, that's what you've got to remember. If your daughter thinks she's too good to come home, then why would you want her there? Change the locks.

Prue   Oh, I just let all that wash over me. All I've got now is my bingo, but my eyes are going, you know? I'll have to stop going out. The kids all make fun of me.

There's a tremendous burst of shouting downstairs.

Prue   What was that?

Bernie   It's a wee experiment. Bare-knuckle fights. The women love it and I take a cut off the betting. But the favourite went down grietin in two minutes at the start of the night. The girls weren't happy. True love thwarted, they're angry now. God help us if another pretty boy loses.

Bernie *goes to the stair door and shouts down.*

Bernie   Penny! (*Deafening.*) *Penny!* First glass in the air, you get those grills down, hear me? Call time early, yeah? Half an hour. (*To* **Prue**.) We had a bit of bother at a wedding thing the other week there. Had to up the security.

Prue   Are you still running those singles nights?

Bernie   Starting again next week. Do better with that in the spring.

Prue   I've got to hand it to you, Bernie, you know how to run the business.

Bernie   Aye, with blood, sweat and tears. Half of them are no single, of course. Cheap shag nights. Always made me money. You want some prawn biryani, Prue?

Prue   Oh, I can't eat. I've only got half my stomach you know.

Thunderous hammering and shouting below. Smashing glass.

Prue   My God! Oh my heart's coming through my ribcage!

Bernie *is running for the door.*

Bernie   Get those grills down! Penny! Get those grills down now! (*Half to herself.*) Christ, they'll tear the place up again. Get the doors open! Get the doors open, let them out!

Bernie *grabs up a baseball bat and runs off.* **Prue** *looks, terrified, at the young women, none of whom even seem interested, still watching TV.*

Shouting below, **Bernie**'s *voice pitched over it.*

Bernie (*offstage*)   That is *time*, ladies and gentlemen! Outside! Outside now! Come on, gents, don't let this mob spoil your drinking. Help me out here! Come on, clear this place out!

Thank you! That's it. Thank you!

A pause, the noise continues but starts to diminish, a crowd moving outside. **Bernie** *reappears upstairs, breathless and dishevelled. She stows the bat.*

Bernie   I'm getting too old for this.

Prue   I don't know how you run this place without a man.

Bernie   Well . . . that's the way it is.

Adie *gets up.*

Bernie   Where do you think you're going?

Adie   I want a drink.

Bernie   There's beer there.

Adie   I want wine.

Bernie   Maggie's on her way to the kitchen anyway.

Maggie *instantly takes the hint and starts clearing plates.*

Maggie   I'll bring the bottle in.

Bernie   There you go, Adie, say thank you to your sister and sit down.

Prue   So when's the wedding?

Bernie   This Saturday.

Prue   You must be so pleased.

Bernie   Come if you like, Prue, it's a big enough do. You're Tony's family after all.

Prue   Oh . . . yes . . . It's just with his health . . .

Bernie   Whatever.

Melly (*to* **Maggie**) You've trod on my make-up mirror! You've broken it!

Maggie   So? We've had our bad luck, haven't we?

Melly   You'll be getting a bit more in a minute!

Bernie   Stop bickering, the pair of you!

Prue (*to* **Agnes**)   Is that the ring, darling?

Agnes (*holding it out*)   You want to see?

Prue   Oh, it's beautiful! Three pearls. Of course in my day pearls meant tears.

Agnes   Oh well, I'm not superstitious.

Adie   Things mean what they mean. Pearls mean tears and diamonds mean love.

Prue   Oh, that's what they say.

Bernie   Pearls, diamonds, you make your own luck in this world.

Marty   But diamonds help.

Prue   It's going to be a big do, you say?

Bernie   Food's setting me back sixteen grand. That's just the food.

Maggie   She's got that new Indian chef, him that was on the telly?

Prue   Oh, I don't think I saw that . . .

Bernie   God mind the do me and Tony had, Prue? Sausage rolls and cava, and we thought we were just the thing.

Prue   Well, it doesn't matter how you start, does it, as long as you're happy.

Adie   Yeah, that's the tricky bit.

Bernie   Everyone's happy here.

A horn outside

Prue (*getting up*)   Oh, that's my cab. (*To* **Agnes**.) Next time I'm over you'll be in your own place.

Bernie   No, no, she'll still be here most of the time. We'll run the business from here.

Pause.

Prue   Anyway . . . you'll have to show me all the photos.

Agnes   I'd love to.

Prue   Goodnight all, lovely to see you again.

Bernie (*staying seated*)   See you, Prue.

A chorus of 'Night, Auntie Prue', 'Cheerio then', from the young women. No one gets up or diverts much attention from the telly.

Prue *leaves.*

Bernie   Christ, I thought she'd never go.

Adie (*getting up*)   I better go and see if she closed the front door properly.

Melly   Don't worry, I'm going.

Adie   The rain's stopped. I thought I might go down to the corner for some chocolate.

Marty   I'll come with you.

Adie   I don't think I'll get lost.

Melly   You need company in the dark.

Adie *glares at them but has to submit.* **Melly**, **Adie** *and* **Marty** *exit.* **Agnes** *is helping* **Maggie** *clear.*

Bernie   Have you made your peace with Marty yet, Agnes? That carry on was just her idea of a sick joke. You should forget it.

Agnes   You know she doesn't like me.

Bernie   I don't know what's in her head. I don't care. She's toeing the line now and that's good enough for me. The family stands together. You hear me?

Agnes   Yes.

Bernie   That's it then.

Maggie   Anyway, you'll soon be shot of the lot of us.

Agnes   But I won't, will I?

Maggie *exits with the plates.*

Bernie   How are things going with Peter? Everyone happy at his end?

Agnes   You talk to his dad more than I do.

Bernie   But what about Peter himself, what does he say?

Agnes   He's a bit . . .

Bernie   What?

Agnes   Distracted. He talks to me as if he's thinking about something else. If I ask him what's wrong he just says, 'Oh, everyone's got problems.'

Bernie   So don't ask him what's wrong. You think I ever asked your father why he was in a black mood? Do you think it would have done me any good to know?

Agnes   Peter's not like Tony.

Bernie   You're telling me. But a new man is still a man and his family's still in the same line of work last time I looked.

Agnes   There's something else, Mum. There's something he's hiding from me.

Bernie   So do you think you'd be happier if you knew what it was? You know where you'll be living and in what style. You know what you can afford, and that's all good news. Pin a smile on your face for the boy, for God's sake. He's sorting us all out.

Agnes   I should be happy, I know, but I'm not.

Bernie   Well, isn't that the story of your life, Agnes?

Agnes   Sometimes I look at Peter and it's like he's fading out – as if he was just a film I was watching and the light was bleaching out of it . . .

Pause.

Bernie   We need to change that prescription you're on, Agnes. I told you.

Agnes   I hope that's it.

Bernie   When are you seeing him again?

Agnes   Not till the wedding. (*Wryly.*) Bad luck to see the bride before the wedding.

Bernie   We've got your luck in order. Don't you worry.

Adie, **Marty** and **Melly** *come back in.*

Melly   It's so dark tonight!

Adie   The street light's out on the corner again. You can't see two steps ahead of yourself.

Marty   A great night for bad men and burglars.

Adie   We saw a swan.

Agnes   What?

Melly   It's true. It must have been flying up to the park. We heard its wings over our heads. Frightening. Like a ghost.

Adie   I felt the air it moved on my face. White. It filled up the darkness.

Marty   This one stood there staring after it till she nearly cricked her neck.

Adie   The sky's clear. No rain. You can even see the stars.

Marty   Oh aye, it's practically the Caribbean out there.

Adie   Didn't you think it was lovely?

Marty   Excuse me for not turning a dirty great bird and a wet wind into a magic moment. Some of us have grown out of daydreams, Adie.

Adie   Christ, that is so typical.

Bernie   You're as bad as each other. Be quiet.

Agnes   Good night.

Melly   You're never going to bed? It's only just turned twelve.

Agnes   I'm tired.

She exits. The other young women exchange looks.

Adie   Mum? I got you this.

She takes something over to **Bernie**.

Bernie   What is it? (*Taking it.*) Turkish delight?

Adie   Princess sweeties.

Marty   What?

Bernie   That's what me and Adie used to call it, when she was wee.

Adie   Mum was going to get me a magic carpet.

Bernie   That bath mat never did get up in the air.

Adie   It's all right. That was all the magic carpet I needed. I've been remembering that, Mum. I'm sorry, Mum.

Bernie   Oh Adie . . . (*She is completely thrown, disarmed.*) Well, we've all been forgetting the old times, haven't we?

Melly   I don't see why anything has to change. I hate it.

Adie   A wee bit of change is good. Like not hearing the rain on the roof. That's good. Can I open a window, Mum? Let some air in now?

Bernie (*opening Turkish delight*) Aye, on you go, pet.

Adie (*leaning out*)   Feel that wind. It's such a beautiful night.

Bernie (*offering Turkish delight*)   You want some of this, Maggie?

Maggie   Too sweet for me.

Marty   Sweet enough to rot your teeth.

Adie *waves the bottles they've bought.*

Adie   Can we have these in your room, Melly? You can see the sky from there.

Melly   Aye, OK.

Bernie   Oh! Oh! Where's mine?

Adie *gives her a bottle.*

Bernie   On you go then, but don't wake your sister.

Melly   Couple of these'll knock me straight out. You know what I'm like.

Maggie   Well, I'm as bad.

Maggie, **Melly** *and* **Adie** *exit.* **Marty** *hesitates, watching* **Bernie**.

Bernie   Go on! Off you go with your sisters. Give me peace.

Marty *exits.*

Bernie *eats Turkish delight and drinks, laughing to herself.*

Bernie   Midnight feasts! God, nothing changes does it?

Adie*'s music starts up overhead.* **Penny** *comes in with wads of cash.*

Penny   Are you still up?

Bernie   Still up, enjoying the peace and quiet, wondering where this terrible disaster you're sure is going to fall on my family might be hiding itself. No trouble here, Penny.

Penny   Bernie, can we just drop that?

Bernie   I told you I knew my own family and I told you my girls knew what was good for them. There's no choices here, no either-or, no yes-or-no, just these eyes, watching everything. They're the answer to every question.

Penny   Looks like you're right, Bernie. You've got them all neatly put away in a drawer. I'm just saying no one can keep an eye on what's happening in here. (*She puts her hand on her chest.*)

Bernie   My girls are breathing quiet enough.

Penny   And what more does a mother need to worry about? Suits me. I've got enough on my plate doing my job and running round after you all.

Bernie   So you're keeping your mouth shut now, are you?

Penny   Like you said, Bernie, I just work here.

Bernie   There you go.

Penny   It's all quiet downstairs now.

Bernie   Good.

Penny   Still, you never know. All it takes is one wee shove.

Bernie   What are you talking about?

Penny   One drink spilled, one dark look in the wrong eyes . . . Trouble can kick off in a second.

Bernie   Is trouble kicking off again downstairs, Penny?

Penny   No. They're happy.

Bernie   Good, then I'm going to bed.

Bernie *exits.* **Penny** *starts sorting notes to put in the wall safe.* **Adie***'s tune plays again upstairs.*

Penny   I can't do any more. I can't do any more. No one can ask it of me. I've told her. I've warned her. She's so full of herself she ties the blindfold over her own eyes. Quiet, is it? There's a thunderstorm waiting in every room of this house. If that storm breaks . . . Well, I've warned her. What else can I do?

As she goes on muttering to herself, **Penny** *gets the safe open and starts stacking the money neatly away.*

There's no love in this house. There's no love here, so why am I here? They'd tear each other's guts out to make puddings. Raised like hyenas. Why should I care?

Stands to reason, stands to reason, send a boy like Peter Romanov into that, with his caring hands and listening ears and caramel eyes promising sweetness for ever. Girls that don't know how to touch a child with caring, girls that don't know what it is to sit on anyone's knee or lean into a shoulder, girls that are crying out to be rescued from their own badness. No one ever gave them honey. They'll cut themselves to pieces smashing the jar to get it all now.

Adie *comes on in her underwear.*

Penny   Are you still up too?

Adie   I thought I heard someone. I wanted to see who it was.

Penny   It's only me.

Adie   You're still working? I thought we shut at twelve tonight.

Penny   I've just this to sort out.

Barking outside.

God save us! Is that the Romanov boy?

Adie   No. He doesn't like the dogs.

Penny   Well, what are the rest of them doing out there tonight? (*Hesitates, then, decisive.*) You go up, Adie, I'll take a look. Check things are OK downstairs. Go on, go back to bed, I'll get your mother if she's needed.

Adie *exits.* **Penny** *follows. She's left the safe open.*

Mary *enters. She is holding a pigeon, stroking it. She's singing, dancing.*

Mary
Sweet feathers, baby blethers,
We're going down to paddle our toes,
The red ladybug is home and snug,
You can sook on my breast till you grow.

Bernie tears your heart out,
Maggie cooks it up,
Sweet feathers (*seagull noise*)
We'll dance on the sand till our mammy calls us home.

Not you, not me, they canny catch us,
The sky's too big to keep us in,
We'll play in the waves
In a wee cockle boat.

Bernie tears your heart out,
Maggie cooks it up,
Sweet feathers (*seagull noise*)
We'll dance on the sand till our mammy calls us home.

Mary *starts trying to climb out of the window, holding the bird. She can't make it.*

Adie *enters as she's struggling. She's still in her underwear. She hesitates as she sees* **Mary**. **Mary** *doesn't notice her.* **Adie** *is carrying a small case. She hides it behind the settee and slips out again.*

Mary *goes on struggling.*

Mary   Oh help me! Why will no one help me?

Marty *comes on.*

Marty   Grandma! Where are you going?

Mary   Are you going to open the door for me? Who are you?

Marty   How did you get out?

Mary   I picked the lock with a kirby grip. Who are you?

Marty   Go back to bed.

Mary   Now I know you. You're the soor plum. Marty the martyr. When are you going to get yourself a bairn? I've got this one.

Marty   Where did you get that?

Mary   I know it's just a seagull. Why can't a seagull be a bairn?

Marty   It's a pigeon.

Mary   It's a baby. A wee bit of life on my windowsill. I grabbed it. Better a wee bit of life than a prune for a womb. Bernie'll tear out your heart, you know, and Maggie'll boil it in Bisto . . .

Marty   Shhh!

Mary   It's the truth! Everything is so dark. You think I can't have babies because I'm dying my hair. Well, I've fooled you. My hair's white like bright sun, like it always was. I don't need the bottle, look at the roots, look! My hair shines white and I can have as many babies as I like. This baby will have white hair and this baby will have another baby and that one will have another, all of us with sun-white hair, we'll be like waves,

one and another and another. And then we'll all sit down with
our white heads and we'll be foam on the sea. Why isn't there
sea foam here? There's no sunlight here.

Marty   Keep it down!

Mary   We kept our doors open. We all kept our doors open,
and when my mother's neighbour had a baby she'd send me
over with a pie or a pan of broth and I'd just walk in the
kitchen, just walk in and see the bonny bairn. Your hair'll go
white but you'll never leave your door open. (*Struggling to climb
out again.*) I have to go, but I'm scared the dogs will bite me.
Will you come with me till I'm through the dark? I don't like
the dark. I like the sun, and Daddy out on the boat and the
doors wide open. Sleeping in Mammy's bed and hearing her
laughing with Daddy through the floor.

There was a boy I saw out the window that smiled like my
daddy. He looked in her face and he kissed her like tasting
sugar on a cake. Will he eat her up? They might eat each
other up, a boy and a girl as sweet as icing sugar . . . they'll
melt in the rain.

Marty (*pulling her away from the window*)   Get away from
there! Go back to bed!

The bird escapes and flies out into the dark.

Mary   That's my bairn. I've lost my baby. I've lost my bit of
life.

Marty   Go back to bed. We'll get it tomorrow. I'll help you
catch it tomorrow.

Mary   No. No. Let it go. You have to let it go.

She starts to cry quietly. She goes off slowly. **Marty** *follows.*

Mary
    Sweet feathers, baby blethers,
    We're going down to paddle our toes,
    The red ladybug is home and snug,
    You can sook on my breast till you grow.

Adie *comes on again, a dress and shoes in her hands. She looks round quickly. Satisfied she's alone, she drops the dress quickly over her head.*

Marty *comes back in.*

Marty Going somewhere, Adie?

Adie (*starting*) Jesus Christ! Thought you were Mum. Leave me alone, Marty.

Adie *is getting her shoes on. Dogs bark outside.*

Marty You're running off with him!

Adie I'm not!

Marty You are! You're getting out!

Adie I'm not! I just . . . Why are you always following me Marty?

Marty *leans out of the window, looking.*

Marty Why are all the dogs running through the dark? What have the Romanovs lost?

Adie Go and ask them.

They face each other down for a moment.

Marty I'm going to shout my lungs out, Adie. I'm stopping you.

Adie You can't. No one can stop me. I'm young, I'm strong, I've got more life in me than you'll ever know. I've seen you all sitting in this room growing mould and acting like excitment's just something you swallow with a vodka chaser. You're dead already. How can you stop me?

Marty He's *weak*! He can't even stand up to his daddy. Daddy says marry sad old Agnes and Petey just says 'When?' and sends roses!

Adie He's just playing them. He never took his eyes off me.

Marty He's marrying Agnes, Adie!

Adie He doesn't love her.

Marty   No! But he'll still go through with it! See what I'm saying?

Adie   He loves me!

Marty   And is he out there now, Adie? Risking everything? Running through the dark and the dogs to take you away?!

Adie *says nothing. She just smiles.*

Marty   I don't believe it.

Marty *looks out of the window again.*

Adie   You wanted him, didn't you? The minute you saw him. You thought you could just turn it on like you always do. 'Look at me, I'm so sick and dark and damaged I'll do any dirty thing you want' – what man can resist that? Well, he did, didn't he, Marty? You don't give a stuff if he marries Agnes. You just can't bear knowing he wanted me and not you.

Marty (*turning on her*)   All right! I'll say it. I don't care if my heart bursts like a rotten orange. All right, I wanted him.

Adie *instantly softens, she tries to hold* **Marty***.*

Adie   Oh Marty, please, it's not my fault. Be happy for me.

Marty   *Happy* for you? Don't touch me! Don't you dare touch me! You think I see my wee sister now? You're just a stupid little girl that thinks she's got fairy wings with stardust on them. I'm going to tear them off and watch you fall.

She pushes **Adie** *away.*

Adie   I can't help you, Marty. If you want to drown, you'll drown. Peter's waiting for me. We're getting on a plane.

Marty   You're not going anywhere.

Adie   You think I could stay here once I'd tasted his mouth? We don't care what happens. His dad can rage. Mum can scream. They can tie me up, set fire to me, beat every drop of blood out of me. They won't be able to kill what's in my eyes when I look at him. We're together now, even if they kill us.

Marty   Oh listen to Juliet! It's a lie, Adie!

Adie   All right. All right, you won't let me go? You're going to wake Mum? Fine. I'll stay. I'll go back up to bed. Peter can marry Agnes on Saturday. What do I care? You just watch Marty, one day, first chance we get, we'll be gone.

Marty   It's not going to happen, Adie, not while there's blood in my body.

Adie   Marty, you can't even get out of bed without swallowing fifteen kinds of pill. The way I feel I could fly straight up through this roof if I wanted to.

Marty   And I'd have your ankles in one fist! You're so sure, you just don't care, do you? I hate you, Adie! I hate you for what you think you can do to us all!

Adie   I thought you'd understand. I thought of all the family you'd know why I had to go. I never knew how much darkness you'd swallowed, Marty, it's all you are now isn't it?

There's a low whistle outside. **Adie** *darts to the window.* **Marty** *grabs her.*

Marty   Where do you think you're going?

Adie   Let go of me!

Marty   I thought you were the strong one, Adie!

Adie   Let go!

They struggle.

Marty   Mum! *Mum!*

Adie   *No!*

Bernie *comes in, carrying her baseball bat.*

Bernie   What's this racket? What's going on? I'll smash you into jam!

Marty (*pushing* **Adie** *away*)   She's got a bag packed! She's running off with Peter Romanov! He's down there waiting on her!

Bernie   You sleekit wee *hoor*!

She rushes at **Adie**

Adie   You can't stop me! You're not my jailer any more!

She grabs the bat off her mother and throws it away.

No more of that! Do you hear me! We're going away. We're getting away from all of you, all the blood and beatings and grubby piles of filthy money.

Maggie *enters.*

Maggie   What's going on? Adie!

Penny *and* **Agnes** *enter.*

Adie   He loves me. Do you know that now, Agnes? Go downstairs now and tell him you know. We're going to fly somewhere we don't even have to think about you all. He's down there now, hear his heart beating? Thumping like mine, for me, Agnes. Me.

Agnes   My God!

Bernie   I'm going to sort that fucker!

She darts to the safe. She snatches out the gun and exits, **Marty** *running after her, cannoning into* **Melly** *who's just entered, terrified.*

Adie *tries to run after them.* **Agnes** *has hold of her.*

Adie   No! Peter! Peter!

Agnes   You're not getting out of here! Look at your stupid Bambi eyes all tears and romance, eh? You're a wee tart! You stole him!

Maggie   Let her go, Agnes. Let her catch her plane. I don't ever want to see her again.

The sound of a shot. They all freeze. After a long moment **Bernie** *comes in, carrying the gun,* **Marty** *close behind.* **Bernie** *puts the gun down.*

Bernie   Let's see if you dare go and look at your boyfriend now.

Marty (*almost laughing, hysterical*)   She did it! I canny believe it!
She finished him!

Adie   No.

She tries to get past them.

Bernie   I've locked the door, Adie. The locks are on all the
windows and I've got the keys. Only place you can go is your
room.

She holds **Adie** *up as she collapses.*

Bernie   Go on, baby. Off to bed.

Adie *starts to leave.* **Penny** *walks into the room. They're all watching*
Bernie. *No one sees* **Adie** *pick up the gun as she exits.*

Penny   You . . . killed Peter Romanov?

Bernie   *No!*

Marty   Bugger made it to his car.

Bernie   I canny help it! Women canny shoot straight.

Maggie   Then why did you say that?!

Marty   Stupid wee cow wants drama? I'll give her drama.
I'd like to pour a river of blood on her head!

Penny   You bitch!

Bernie   Look. It's better if that's what Adie thinks. We're
going to have to have a meeting first thing, Agnes, you, me
and Daddy Romanov. He's in the wrong. He'll know fine he
was in the wrong, couldn't keep his own boy on a lead! Adie's
just a baby, we'll tell him . . .

There's the sound of a gunshot upstairs.

Bernie   Adie?! Adie?!

She flies out of the room.

Penny   Oh Christ, no.

Melly (*in a whisper*)   What is it?

Bernie *screams overhead, a long howl of loss and anguish.* **Penny** *runs out of the room.*

Bernie (*offstage*)   Oh my baby! My baby!

Melly *starts to cry quietly.* **Marty** *staggers.*

Bernie *comes on, carrying* **Adie**'s *body. Blood.* **Bernie** *is mad with grief and shock.*

Bernie   Look what she's done! The wee bitch! Look what she's done to hersel! Oh how could she! How could she! Look what she's done to me!

Penny *is close behind her.*

Penny (*quietly, urgent*)   Police and ambulance, Maggie, quick.

Bernie   She's spoiled hersel! She's spoiled everything! Oh God, it's all gone! Oh, how could she!

Penny   Quick as you like, Maggie!

Maggie *gets on the phone, shaky, asking for police and ambulance under this.* **Bernie** *has put* **Adie**'s *body down. She turns away from her.*

Bernie   I can't look at her! I won't look at her. I'll kill him. Peter Romanov, you run away with your life into the dark, over the sea, but we'll find you, one day we'll find you!

Slowly the women apart from **Marty** *gather round* **Bernie**. *The scene is transforming.* **Adie** *is carried off. The women are transforming* **Bernie**, *cleaning the blood off her, changing her clothes, doing hair and make-up.* **Bernie** *talks through all of this.*

Bernie   We can still fix this, we can still fix it. Agnes, set up a meeting with Mr Romanov. Oh God, I'll kill his son. I'll have to shoot him. We can still save this. They're to blame. Oh my baby . . .

Marty (*looking after* **Adie**)   She was smiling . . .

Bernie   Be quiet! My nerves are . . . My nerves are just . . . I can do this. I can hold it together. Shut up! Nobody cry! We've got to hold this together or we'll all drown!

The **Careworker** *is on, she's crying.*

Bernie   She was my baby. I didn't know. I couldn't know. None of us knew. Understand? None of us knew . . . (*Hears* **Careworker**.) What are you bawling about?!

Careworker   Oh Mrs Alba, I'm so sorry for your loss.

Bernie *is completely pulled together now. Cold and steely.*

Bernie   Get out of here with your tears. Who are you to cry for my daughter? Who are you? Make yourself useful. Let them in.

The **Careworker** *exits.* **Bernie** *is arranging herself.*

Bernie   Hankie.

Maggie *hands her a cloth hankie.*

Bernie   Girls.

The young women, apart from **Marty**, *arrange themselves around* **Bernie**.

Bernie   No sobbing. Hear me, Maggie? We're going to hold this together.

The Camera Crew and Interviewer are ushered in by the **Careworker**.

Bernie (*sharp whisper*)   Marty!

Slowly **Marty** *joins the tableau round* **Bernie**.

The lights go on. **Bernie** *bows her head and then looks up into the camera lens.*

Bernie   The whole family is just devastated. My daughter was so young and full of life. We just can't understand how this could have happened. I can't believe my baby's gone. We're just an ordinary happy family. She was just an ordinary happy teenager. Nobody could have seen this coming. Nobody. (*Pause.*) That's it.

Blackout.

Methuen Drama Student Editions

Jean Anouilh *Antigone* • John Arden *Serjeant Musgrave's Dance*
Alan Ayckbourn *Confusions* • Aphra Behn *The Rover* • Edward Bond
Lear • *Saved* • Bertolt Brecht *The Caucasian Chalk Circle* • *Fear and
Misery in the Third Reich* • *The Good Person of Szechwan* • *Life of Galileo* •
Mother Courage and her Children • *The Resistible Rise of Arturo Ui* • *The
Threepenny Opera* • Anton Chekhov *The Cherry Orchard* • *The Seagull* •
Three Sisters • *Uncle Vanya* • Caryl Churchill *Serious Money* • *Top Girls*
• Shelagh Delaney *A Taste of Honey* • Euripides *Elektra* • *Medea* •
Dario Fo *Accidental Death of an Anarchist* • Michael Frayn *Copenhagen*
• John Galsworthy *Strife* • Nikolai Gogol *The Government Inspector* •
Robert Holman *Across Oka* • Henrik Ibsen *A Doll's House* • *Ghosts* •
Hedda Gabler • Charlotte Keatley *My Mother Said I Never Should* •
Bernard Kops *Dreams of Anne Frank* • Federico García Lorca *Blood
Wedding* • *Doña Rosita the Spinster* (bilingual edition) • *The House of
Bernarda Alba* • (bilingual edition) • *Yerma* (bilingual edition) • David
Mamet *Glengarry Glen Ross* • *Oleanna* • Patrick Marber *Closer* • John
Marston *Malcontent* • Martin McDonagh *The Lieutenant of Inishmore* •
Joe Orton *Loot* • Luigi Pirandello *Six Characters in Search of an Author*
• Mark Ravenhill *Shopping and F***ing* • Willy Russell *Blood Brothers*
• *Educating Rita* • Sophocles *Antigone* • *Oedipus the King* • Wole
Soyinka *Death and the King's Horseman* • Shelagh Stephenson *The
Memory of Water* • August Strindberg *Miss Julie* • J. M. Synge *The
Playboy of the Western World* • Theatre Workshop *Oh What a Lovely
War* Timberlake Wertenbaker *Our Country's Good* • Arnold Wesker
The Merchant • Oscar Wilde *The Importance of Being Earnest* •
Tennessee Williams *A Streetcar Named Desire* • *The Glass Menagerie*

Methuen Drama Modern Plays

include work by

Edward Albee
Jean Anouilh
John Arden
Margaretta D'Arcy
Peter Barnes
Sebastian Barry
Brendan Behan
Dermot Bolger
Edward Bond
Bertolt Brecht
Howard Brenton
Anthony Burgess
Simon Burke
Jim Cartwright
Caryl Churchill
Noël Coward
Lucinda Coxon
Sarah Daniels
Nick Darke
Nick Dear
Shelagh Delaney
David Edgar
David Eldridge
Dario Fo
Michael Frayn
John Godber
Paul Godfrey
David Greig
John Guare
Peter Handke
David Harrower
Jonathan Harvey
Iain Heggie
Declan Hughes
Terry Johnson
Sarah Kane
Charlotte Keatley
Barrie Keeffe
Howard Korder

Robert Lepage
Doug Lucie
Martin McDonagh
John McGrath
Terrence McNally
David Mamet
Patrick Marber
Arthur Miller
Mtwa, Ngema & Simon
Tom Murphy
Phyllis Nagy
Peter Nichols
Sean O'Brien
Joseph O'Connor
Joe Orton
Louise Page
Joe Penhall
Luigi Pirandello
Stephen Poliakoff
Franca Rame
Mark Ravenhill
Philip Ridley
Reginald Rose
Willy Russell
Jean-Paul Sartre
Sam Shepard
Wole Soyinka
Simon Stephens
Shelagh Stephenson
Peter Straughan
C. P. Taylor
Theatre de Complicite
Theatre Workshop
Sue Townsend
Judy Upton
Timberlake Wertenbaker
Roy Williams
Snoo Wilson
Victoria Wood

Methuen Drama Contemporary Dramatists
include

John Arden (two volumes)
Arden & D'Arcy
Peter Barnes (three volumes)
Sebastian Barry
Dermot Bolger
Edward Bond (eight volumes)
Howard Brenton
(two volumes)
Richard Cameron
Jim Cartwright
Caryl Churchill (two volumes)
Sarah Daniels (two volumes)
Nick Darke
David Edgar (three volumes)
David Eldridge
Ben Elton
Dario Fo (two volumes)
Michael Frayn (three volumes)
David Greig
John Godber (four volumes)
Paul Godfrey
John Guare
Lee Hall (two volumes)
Peter Handke
Jonathan Harvey
(two volumes)
Declan Hughes
Terry Johnson (three volumes)
Sarah Kane
Barrie Keeffe
Bernard-Marie Koltès
(two volumes)
Franz Xaver Kroetz
David Lan
Bryony Lavery
Deborah Levy
Doug Lucie

David Mamet (four volumes)
Martin McDonagh
Duncan McLean
Anthony Minghella
(two volumes)
Tom Murphy (six volumes)
Phyllis Nagy
Anthony Neilsen (two volumes)
Philip Osment
Gary Owen
Louise Page
Stewart Parker (two volumes)
Joe Penhall (two volumes)
Stephen Poliakoff
(three volumes)
David Rabe (two volumes)
Mark Ravenhill (two volumes)
Christina Reid
Philip Ridley
Willy Russell
Eric-Emmanuel Schmitt
Ntozake Shange
Sam Shepard (two volumes)
Wole Soyinka (two volumes)
Simon Stephens (two volumes)
Shelagh Stephenson
David Storey (three volumes)
Sue Townsend
Judy Upton
Michel Vinaver
(two volumes)
Arnold Wesker (two volumes)
Michael Wilcox
Roy Williams (three volumes)
Snoo Wilson (two volumes)
David Wood (two volumes)
Victoria Wood

Methuen Drama World Classics

include

Jean Anouilh (two volumes)
Brendan Behan
Aphra Behn
Bertolt Brecht (eight volumes)
Büchner
Bulgakov
Calderón
Čapek
Anton Chekhov
Noël Coward (eight volumes)
Feydeau
Eduardo De Filippo
Max Frisch
John Galsworthy
Gogol
Gorky (two volumes)
Harley Granville Barker
(two volumes)
Victor Hugo
Henrik Ibsen (six volumes)
Jarry

Lorca (three volumes)
Marivaux
Mustapha Matura
David Mercer (two volumes)
Arthur Miller (five volumes)
Molière
Musset
Peter Nichols (two volumes)
Joe Orton
A. W. Pinero
Luigi Pirandello
Terence Rattigan
(two volumes)
W. Somerset Maugham
(two volumes)
August Strindberg
(three volumes)
J. M. Synge
Ramón del Valle-Inclan
Frank Wedekind
Oscar Wilde

For a complete catalogue
of Methuen Drama titles
write to:

Methuen Drama
36 Soho Square
London W1D 3QY

or you can visit our website at:

www.methuendrama.com